AF449466

Frontispiece and tailpiece:
Olav Westphalen, *Untitled* (2008)

This publication was realized with generous support of
KU-Project funding from Kungl. Konsthögskolan,
The Royal Institute of Art, Stockholm, Sweden.

Axl Books, Stockholm, 2015
www.axlbooks.com
info@axlbooks.com

ISBN 978-91-86883-33-1

Ignorance

Between Knowing
and Not Knowing

Gavin Morrison
Sigrid Sandström
(editors)

AXL BOOKS

Contents

We Are Ignorant

Gavin Morrison
Sigrid Sandström

IGNORANCE IS ENDEMIC; it is talked of like it is a disease or affliction with the attended suggestion that it can be caught and transferred to others. The dunce sitting in the corner is a gesture of quarantine, not simply punishment. There is a moral dimension to ignorance. Ignorance is not merely not knowing; there is a presumption that the absent knowledge *should* be known, thereby ignorance is a defective or incomplete form of the normative state. Choosing ignorance is an obstinate refusal to comply, a renegade mode that refuses to defer to standards of knowledge. However, this requires the individual to be aware of their ignorance, knowing that one does not know. The necessity of this structural relationship is paralleled within various art making practices. Indeed, those who would most commonly be thought of as ignorant are referred to as naïve artists. Their ignorance which sets them apart. They are likely unaware of their naïvety, and their failing in relation to the standard methods or techniques. However, this publication considers ignorance in relation to creative practices in the widest sense in which ignorance is more nuanced and pervasive than commonly perceived.

In a sense, this book provides a minor corrective to the academicization of art practice and the compulsion to determine metrics for appraisal and accreditation. It is frequently assumed that art practice aspires to knowledge. While certain approaches may have such aspirations, other methodologies eschew such an objective. We are frequently confronted with anecdotes that suggest that the artist orbits the limits of knowledge and that resolution is not attained by the discovery of truth but the act of discovering. Artists often claim to be asking questions, rather than seeking answers. This committed, non-teleological approach provides liberation from the tyranny of absolutism. However, how is this position to be maintained with any form of criticality without the attendant structures that knowledge affords? In this light, it is appropriate to consider the modes in which ignorance exists within art as well as a broader cultural setting.

In his essay, JOHN LLEWELYN distinguishes between the verbal application of "ignore" and nominal ignorance, where the former is actively choosing not to consider something while the latter is a state of not knowing. This distinction is a fruitful way to consider the instances described by ELLINOR HÅLLÉN in which an artist assumes a naïvety within their approach. Her example of Jackson Pollock's action painting can appear as a faux-naïvety or willful ignorance, which ignores a convention or teaching. In contrast, outsider artists' ignorance lacks such a motive. Similarly, JONNA BORNEMARK describes instructing two groups of students, one group was composed of high achievers and the other of students unfamiliar with advanced study, on a difficult passage of philosophy. Both groups were ignorant of the meaning of the text. However, the latter group approached the text with a generosity of potential where their failure to understand was not unexpected, while the former group of students were crippled by their expectations of being able to understand. For Bornemark, this could be considered as sympathetic with the alterity exposed through the doxic bracketing of the phenomenological reduction, where those who did not expect to understand can see their ignorance as the expected product of the otherness of the experience. This conception of the self allows for a productive ignorance. This ignorance would seem to be a necessary condition for the critical engagement of art, where ignorance is tolerated. Although knowledge may provide benefits and insights, it can be a limiting factor if relied upon too heavily.

BARRY SCHWABSKY draws attention to the functional necessity of a "someone else" for a work to be completed; artistic work requires a viewer, which introduces the possibility that this viewer might possess an awareness of the work that the artist lacks. Although an artist may appear as an authority with an omnipotent perspective, both fallibility and deception are often present. The ignorance of the artist can be exposed by the knowledge of the viewer. However, because art is fictive, or at least inventive, such "errors" remain ambiguous and the viewer might attribute significance unintended by the artist.

Knowledge occupies an uncertain position within art, where philosophy could be characterized as the pursuit of knowledge – the banishment of ignorance – art lacks the purity that this functional compulsion bestows. For certain philosophical approaches within the classical tradition, the essentially mimetic aspect of art distinguishes it from philosophy and affords it a proximity to ignorance. Plato's republic expels all imitative poets. For Plato, imitation is problematic because the world is already a representation of ideal forms. Therefore, the imitative poet imitates an imitation (although Plato's comments concern poets, these can be extended to other forms of art). Poets create representations that can also misrepresent; this potential – or fallibility –made poetry morally problematic for Plato. Because poetry is not a method for acquiring knowledge, it necessarily allows ignorance to exist, at a minimum, as an attendant risk. However, for Aristotle, art was potentially capable of conveying knowledge. He contrasted art with history, where the subject of history was the story of a single individual, while the subject of art was universal. Even a work of art concerning a singular character concerned man in the abstract. Therefore, for Aristotle, art was more philosophical than history in its attention to the general and universal. Between these positions, there is ambiguity, which can represent the schism that Nietzsche perceived in humanity striving to retain uncertainty while pursuing the prosaic truths of science. He writes, "How we have known from the start to hold on to our ignorance in order to enjoy a barely comprehensible freedom, thoughtlessness, recklessness, bravery, and joy in life; to delight in life itself! And, until now, science could arise only on this solidified, granite foundation of ignorance."[1] Art occupies this realm of ignorance; it is a

                                        WE ARE IGNORANT

struggle within this "barely comprehensible freedom." This fervent compulsion to ignorance implies that even when artists make factual claims, such as when striving for the definitive objectivity witnessed in the conceptual art in the late 1960s, they are conditioned by this epistemological heritage.

This ambiguity is often deployed within fiction, where the role of the author as the authority is a conspicuous force. ANDREW BENNETT'S essay emphasizes the peculiarities of the narrator as the apparent voice of the author but that is known to be fictional. A narrator declaring ignorance is the expression of a contradiction and failure. Ignorance implies the inability to tell the story one claims to be recounting, but, of course, the story is being told with voiced ambiguity. Arising from this ambiguity is a question about the relationship between the author and narrator, where both inhabit this space of not knowing. Bennett illustrates the resulting uncertainty that this ambiguity provokes using the following quotation from Derrida: "you can take interest in what I am doing here only insofar as you would be right to believe that – *somewhere* – I do not know what I am doing."[2] The author directly addresses the reader and proclaims ignorance of his activity, which is not merely a confession but also a declaration that the reader is required to believe. The author and the reader are both ignorant despite their different types of ignorance.

The function of language within the masking and revelation of ignorance is central to JEANINE OLESON'S libretto for an experimental opera which was staged at the New Museum in New York in 2014. In this publication Oleson represents extracts of the libretto, a reclaiming of textual meaning where the performance allows for dissolving and uncertainty of sense. With this form of articulation of the libretto there is a realignment of the textual author-ity which makes explicit the permeable nature of the rela-tionship between text and performance.

In *The Ignorant Schoolmaster*, philosopher Jacques Rancière argues for a level of parity within the student-teacher rela-tionship in which both lack knowledge rather than the expected dominance of the knowledgeable teacher over the ignorant student. In his essay, KIM WEST considers the significance of ignorance in the title of Rancière's book. West perceives a strategic function of the claim that both the teacher and student are ignorant, which is to create the potential for a new pedagogical model. Mutual ignorance is not merely methodologically expedient; this claim incorporates the political dimension, through flattening the usual pedagogic hierarchy it democratizes learning.

There is undoubtedly a moral dimension to ignorance, which GAVIN MORRISON makes mention of in his essay concerning James Ferrier. Ferrier perceived ignorance as a defect, and as such, we can be blameworthy when we display it. Culpability for one's ignorance implies psycho-logical repercussions. When we do not know what we are expected to know, there exists a sense of shame and the possibility of ridicule. Yet, the knowledge we are expected to know is not universal. Certainly, age and circumstance provide insulation from blame. Through the process of gaining knowledge, naïvety and innocence give way to ignorance. The process mirrors the erosion of ignorance as it yields to knowledge. To retain ignorance is defiant, disruptive of normative expectations, but it is also a pervasive presence, which casts shadows across art in creation and reception.

NOTES

1. Friedrich Nietzsche, *Beyond Good and Evil*
    (Cambridge: Cambridge University Press, 2003),
    p. 25.
2. Cited by Andrew Bennett, "'An Element of Blank':
    On Literary Ignorance" in this volume page 86.

Undecidable Intentions

Barry Schwabsky

IN SPEAKING OF art and ignorance, we should first of all ask, Whose ignorance? The artist's or someone else's? Let us (following Lawrence Weiner) call this someone else *the receiver*. The receiver might be a critic ("Everybody's a critic!"), a collector, a curator, or just a member of that mythical Leviathan, the public. But to be a critic, or indeed, to be a member of the public at all, implies that one might consider oneself to know something about the artist of which the artist is ignorant. The ordinary or educated viewer brings to the work of art something that the artist could not have anticipated, something of which the artist was ignorant, and this is why, as Marcel Duchamp said and as I never tire of repeating, the viewer completes the work.

If this is so, then ignorance is in some sense integral to what we call art. But not just any ignorance. Presumably there are forms of ignorance that are just pernicious. When we become interested in art, we want to know more about it, not less, and we want to know more about the world that it refers to as well. Broadly speaking, we assume that knowing more helps artists to make better art and helps art lovers to appreciate it more. On the other hand, some forms of ignorance may be neutral in their effect on art, or in any case their effect may be artistically indeterminate. Take a simple example from literature. In the opening lines of Franz Kafka's "The Stoker" (the first chapter of the unfinished novel most commonly known in English as *Amerika*), the protagonist, Karl Rossmann, is on a ship entering New York Harbor. He catches sight of the Statue of Liberty, noticing the sword in her upraised hand.

But wait a minute. Liberty doesn't really carry a sword, does she? No. Take a boat ride through New York Harbor and you will see that Liberty carries a torch, not a sword. Illumination is her thing, not violence. When I first read Kafka as a young man, I thought this belligerent Liberty was one of his amazing oneiric inventions, like the inexplicable transformation of Gregor Samsa into an insect; or the appearance of the Odradek, that strange creature that at first "looks like a flat star-shaped spool for thread, and indeed it does seem to have thread wound upon it; to be sure, they are only old, broken-off bits of thread, knotted and tangled together, of the most varied sorts and colors. But it is not only a spool, for a small wooden crossbar sticks out of the middle of the star, and another small rod is joined to that at a right angle"[1]; or even simply of Josef K.'s discovery that the court to which he has been summoned is in the attic of a tenement building. Later, as I began to read more about Kafka, I found out otherwise: Far from representing one of the writer's inspired imaginative leaps, it was simply a mistake, the result of his ignorance: Kafka, who did not know much at all about the United States, simply thought he was accurately describing the famous statue. Luckily, perhaps, my own ignorance about Kafka at the time was perfectly

                    UNDECIDABLE INTENTIONS

complementary to his own, and it allowed me to savor this striking detail as one more example of his genius.

But what should I think now? Is it that the opening paragraph of "The Stoker" is less brilliant than I imagined? Not necessarily in a bad way, mind you, but perhaps simply different. One might simply say that I had misunderstood the function of the paragraph, which was not to immediately announce to the reader that this is going to be a tale in which odd things are likely to occur; quite the opposite, it might be that the paragraph was intended rather to draw the reader in by its very mundaneness, seducing the reader, one might say, into thinking that he was about to read a tale of humdrum realism, the better to pull the rug out from under him later. This interpretation is supported, perhaps, by the rather tawdry reason the paragraph gives for Karl's journey: his parents have sent him to America to separate him from the servant girl whom he has impregnated. We could well be in the world of what one prim and priggish late nineteenth century critic called "that unnecessarily faithful portrayal of offensive incidents for which M. Zola has found the new name of 'Naturalism.'"[2] If the latter is true, then Kafka's ignorance betrayed him; he inadvertently provided a different kind of opening than he intended.

But maybe not. It would also be possible to argue that Kafka's ignorance here, perhaps it would be better to say, his willingness to keep faith with his ignorance, was part and parcel of his brilliance. After all, Kafka was well aware that he knew little about the New World. He must have chosen to write about it precisely because of the freedom it offered him to create a landscape nearly from scratch. He knew that, as the critic Clarence Brown says, "nothing liberates the comic imagination like ignorance."[3] It's not even that he was fantasizing about America, writing just after the death of Karl May, he was fantasizing about European fantasies of America. America, which that American transplanted to Europe, Henry James, anatomized with great vim as a place with "no State, in the European sense of the word, and indeed barely a specific national name. No sovereign, no court, no personal loyalty, no aristocracy, no church, no clergy, no army, no diplomatic service, no country gentlemen, no palaces, no castles." Kafka would have appreciated the lack of castles in particular and the vast scope for ignorance in general in a society in which there was also, as James continues, "No Oxford, nor Eton, nor Harrow; no literature, no novels, no museums, no pictures."[4]

If Kafka's book had been taken in hand during his lifetime by a modern-style editor, he would have been asked whether he wanted to correct his description or maintain it in the face of the facts. We might then feel we had a clearer sense of Kafka's intention, though the intention thus registered would be a retrospective one and not necessarily congruent with what the author was thinking when he first set down the passage. But elsewhere, Kafka's friend and literary executor, Max Brod, did correct some of Kafka's mistakes. For instance, at the end of what we now usually call *Amerika*, when Karl encounters the Nature Theater of Oklahoma: Kafka's manuscript spells the western state's name as "Oklahama" which might make it sound as though its name were half-American, half-Japanese. But actually the misspelling has a very specific source: It seems that Kafka based his understanding of American life and landscape on a picture book called *Amerika Heute und Morgen* by Arthur Holitscher, which was published in 1912. The typographical error "Oklahama" occurs in that book, as Howard Caygill has pointed out, in the caption for a photograph of a lynching: "Oklahama idyll," reads the awful legend. Caygill undoubtedly goes too far in implying that Kafka deliberately repeated Holitscher's typo in order to "carefully preserve" it "to alert readers to his source."[5] Kafka could be a mystifying writer, but he did not set puzzles in this fashion. Besides, if Kafka had intended his apparent mistake to be seen as a deliberate clue, then he was woefully mistaken since the clue seems to have taken nearly a century to be noticed, a real case of ignorance if there ever was one.

Still, awareness of Kafka's source gives pause. And one imagines that if only Brod had known of it, he might have thought better of correcting his friend's error, just in case there really was an important clue secreted in the substitution of "a" for "o." The potentially sinister nature of the utopia offered by the Nature Theatre of Oklahoma (as the standard transcription would have it) is clear from the threatening undertone of its enthusiastic offer:

> If you miss this opportunity, there will never
> be another! Anyone thinking of his future,
> your place is with us! All welcome! Anyone

who wants to be an artist, step forward! We
are the theatre that has a place for everyone,
everyone in his place! If you decide to join us,
we congratulate you here and now! But hurry,
be sure not to miss the midnight deadline!
We shut down at midnight, never to reopen!
Accursed be anyone who doesn't believe us![6]

Perhaps there should be two versions of Kafka's novel, the Oklahoma version and the Oklahama version, one in which the Theatre really is a paradise on earth and one in which it is, as Caygill claims, "more appropriately described in terms of [Hannah] Arendt's description of a concentration camp in the *Origins of Totalitarianism* than as a democratic utopia."[7] And in English, at least, these two versions exist: The first would be the translation from which I have been quoting by Michael Hoffman, which was first published in 1996, which follows the earlier one by Willa and Edwin Muir in retaining Brod's "Oklahoma," while a more recent version by Ritchie Robertson, adheres to the manuscript's use of "Oklahama." However, for Robertson, despite everything , "the Theatre of Oklahoma stands for art as a means of salvation that may continue to be valid after traditional religion has ceased to be credible."[8] The simultaneity of the two versions forms the material representation of our ignorance as to which is the correct interpretation. It's not even clear that, as Caygill seems to think, our choice of interpretations must depend on our belief as to Kafka's intention-more specifically, our belief as to whether he was aware or ignorant of the

UNDECIDABLE INTENTIONS

correct spelling of "Oklahoma." One might as well say of him something like what Quentin Meillassoux has said of Stéphane Mallarmé, that "There is a strong possibility that Mallarmé basically knew no more than we do about his poem, and even that he did not wish to know more; and this is because the Poem is in itself, in fact, a 'machine' for hypotheses-a machine that functions without him, indifferent to his innermost conviction."[9]

In Meillassoux's account, Mallarmé encoded within *Un Coup de dés* a principal of numerical ordering that would be compensatory for the loss of the old poetic functions of meter. But in concealing this numerical order so deeply within his text, the poet was making a wager on whether it would ever be noticed. In other words, Mallarmé was writing in knowing ignorance (a wonderful oxymoron) as to whether the text's secret would ever be discovered. And more than that: Mallarmé might deliberately have been writing in such a way, according to Meillassoux, as to leave the reader in eternal ignorance as to whether the numerical pattern discovered in the text had been deliberately planted there or not. One's choice as to interpretation can only involve a leap of faith or, in Mallarméan terms, a throw of the dice.

In any case, Kafka (like Mallarmé) leaves us face to face with our fundamental ignorance, and with our ignorance as to the extent of his ignorance. But to reach this kind of ignorance, one must have learned a great deal. What the work of a Mallarmé or a Kafka fundamentally is or means in many ways depends on what we bring to it, and the more knowledge we can bring to it, the more crucial our sense of ignorance becomes. This realization could be a provisional conclusion of sorts, but before concluding this essay, and because it is probably expected of me as an art critic, I want give some indication of how ignorance can function in understanding works of plastic art as well as of literature. Since what I am proposing is really an explication of Duchamp's dictum that the viewer completes the work, let us think for a moment about this near-contemporary of Kafka's.

You may recall that in the late 1990s the artist Rhonda Roland Shearer, in collaboration with her late husband, the paleontologist and writer Stephen Jay Gould, made some remarkable claims based on intensive research they had done into Duchamp's readymades. Their proposition, in short, was that there were never really any Duchampian readymades-that all the objects he presented as such were things made by hand by him (or, in the case of what Duchamp acknowledged as "assisted readymades," that the "assistance" had gone far beyond what Duchamp had claimed)[10] Unsurprisingly, Shearer's claims have had (as far as I can tell) little if any effect on the subsequent literature.

But direct refutation of Shearer's evidence is hard to come by. It is also difficult not to suspect that the experts might have been blinded by their unwillingness to contemplate the possibility that their expertise might have been based on ignorance. Besides, the questions that would arise from taking Shearer's ideas seriously are in

    UNDECIDABLE INTENTIONS

many ways more intriguing than those that normally circulate around Duchamp's oeuvre, since they relocate the idea of the readymade for the first time to a truly "conceptual" realm, that is, if Shearer is right, then the readymade was truly an idea and not a thing. So let us just for a moment make a Mallarméan toss of the dice and bet on Shearer. What then? Just as Caygill's idea of a deliberate but hidden Kafkaesque reference to Holitscher's *Amerika Heute und Morgen* or Meillassoux's idea of a deliberate but hidden (and, moreover, deliberately ambiguous) numerical substructure in *Un Coup de dés*, we would have to decide whether Duchamp had, in essence, "forged" his readymades in order to be found out, or whether instead he had done so on the assumption that his imposture (if that's what it is) would never be discovered or, if discovered, the truth of this discovery ever be credited. Duchamp was no stranger to imposture, after all. For decades he claimed (and everyone believed) that he had renounced art in favor of chess and just breathing; after his death, it was discovered that he had all along been working assiduously on Étant donnés. In this case, we can assume that he did want his deception to become known. But if his original *Fountain* was really the work of his own hands, we will probably never know for sure, nor ever know for sure whether we were meant to find him out. Is the fate of a work ever the one we intend for it? In the undecidability of an intention opens the abyss that may be synonymous with what we call art, a "machine for hypotheses." Now, anyone who wants to be an art critic, step forward.

NOTES

1. Franz Kafka, "The Cares of a Family Man," in *The Complete Stories*, ed. Nahum H. Glatzer (New York: Schocken Books, 1995), p. 428.

2. Quoted by Raymond Williams in *Keywords: A Vocabulary of Culture and Society* (London: Fontana, 1983), p. 218.

3. http://www.princeton.edu/~cb/kafka.html

4. Quoted by George Steiner in *George Steiner: A Reader* (New York: Oxford University Press, 1984), p. 105.

5. Howard Caygill, "The Fate of the Pariah: Arendt and Kafka's "Nature Theatre of Oklahama," *College Literature* XXXVIII 1 (Winter 2011).

6. Franz Kafka, *Amerika: The Man Who Disappeared*, transl. Michael Hofmann (New York: New Directions, 2002), p. 202.

7. Caygill, *op. cit.*

8. Franz Kafka, *The Man Who Disappeared (America)*, tr. by Ritchie Robertson (Oxford: Oxford University Press, 2012), p. x

9. Quentin Meillassoux, *The Number and the Siren: A Decipherment of Mallarmé's Coup de dés*, transl. Robin Mackay (Falmouth, UK: Urbanomic, 2012), p. 147. See also my review, "The Most Beautiful Perhaps," *Hyperallergic* (October 7, 2012), http://hyperallergic.com/58076/the-most-beautiful-perhaps/

10. See, for instance, Leslie Camhi, "Did Duchamp Deceive Us?," *Artnews* (February 1999), pp. 98-102.

What Does Ignorance Signify
in Jacques Rancière's
The Ignorant Schoolmaster?

Kim West

THE IGNORANT SCHOOLMASTER, Jacques Rancière's philosophical account of the adventures and misadventures of Joseph Jacotot, an early 19th century pedagogical thinker and experimentalist, is one of the most widely read books in the philosopher's *oeuvre*. It has been translated into many languages, and its influence can be traced within disciplines ranging from philosophy and pedagogics to political science and contemporary art, which is remarkable given its puzzling, undecidable nature. It is a book that seems to resist immediate categorization. Throughout the length of its argument it maintains an insecurity regarding who speaks and for what exact purpose. It seems to generate problems and contradictions rather than offering clear explications or solutions.

The first contradiction the reader encounters is in the title, *The Ignorant Schoolmaster*. This syntagm sets up a blatant paradox that contradicts our basic ideas of what constitutes teaching. How can a *schoolmaster*, that is, a teacher, be *ignorant*, when the very task of teaching – surely, no one would deny – is to transmit *knowledge*, that is, the opposite of ignorance? Are we not currently plagued, in the ongoing crisis of the public school system, by this exact problem: the lack of *qualified*, that is, knowledgeable and well-educated teachers? While we might disagree about the causes of this problem (some would point to a lack of insight regarding the characteristics and needs of the current job market, while others would claim that it has to do with the gradual disintegration of the very notion of education, *Bildung*) the symptoms seem indisputable. Behind these questions – which, as we will see, are to some extent misguided, at least according to the argument of Rancière's book – there lies another, more fundamental one: *what does "ignorance" signify in The Ignorant Schoolmaster?*

This question can be answered in several ways. Here, I provide three versions, each of which is in itself inconclusive, and all of which partly overlap, or even mutually reinforce one another.

1. The question may be addressed on an anecdotal level. Recall the first scene of the book (which may, incidentally, be described as the foundational scene of Rancière's entire philosophical project). Joseph Jacotot, an ambitious young man of many talents, is in exile in the Netherlands, having fled France during the Bourbon Restoration. Due to his loyal service to the republic, Jacotot is graciously offered a teaching position at the University of Leuven. His classes are popular among the students, and he is asked to extend his range of subjects. One group of students wish to learn French. Jacotot wants to accommodate them, but he does not speak Dutch. The instructor and students thus have no common language in which to communicate. As an industrious, adventurous man, Jacotot does not want to

be restrained by his ignorance, and he therefore decides to conduct an experiment. He distributes a book written in French, François Fénelon's *Les Aventures de Télémaque*, printed with a parallel Dutch translation. Through an interpreter, he tells the students, "learn the French text with the help of the translation." Specifically, to "repeat what they had learned over and over, and then [...] read through the rest of the [first] book until they could recite it."[1]

To his great astonishment, the experiment seems to work. The students, having performed the prescribed exercises, demonstrate a remarkable mastery of French. "[H]ow surprised he was," writes Rancière, "to discover that the students, left to themselves, managed this difficult step as well as many French could have done!"[2] In other words, the students were on their way to learning an unknown language *without* the instructor mastering their language and, consequently, without a guide in the learning process that leads from ignorance to knowledge. In fact, Jacotot's ignorance of the Dutch language seems to have been the *condition* for the rapid and effective way in which the students acquired French. Their advancement, he noted, was simply astounding. But what did this mean? Confronted with this situation, explains Rancière, Jacotot had a veritable revelation, that forced him to question his most basic ideas of what constitutes teaching. "Was wanting all that was necessary for doing?", he wondered. "Were all men virtually capable of understanding what others had done and understood?"[3]

Jacotot would go on to systematize this experiment, transforming it into a universal pedagogical method applicable to any field of human understanding. In its most reduced version, the method consists of three steps. First, constrain the student and force her/him to attempt to understand an unknown object (the French text) by comparing it to something s/he knows (the Dutch text). Second, control that the student devotes her/his full attention to this task, by making her/him repeat the unknown object in her/his language, explain what s/he thinks about it, and account for how s/he relates to it, constantly verifying that s/he pays full attention to the unknown object. Third, make the student realize that this work of understanding is evidence of a universal equality of intelligences, that is, of everyone's equal intellectual capacity – and that, therefore, s/he can help anyone come to the same understanding by applying the same method on her/himself, and so on. For Jacotot, this was a universal method of education but also, and perhaps more importantly, a method of intellectual *emancipation*, carrying with it an inherent ideal of equality. And Jacotot's ignorance of the Dutch language was the direct, empirical cause of the development of his method.

2. The above description, however, also suggests something else: that ignorance operates on other levels in Rancière's text. In fact, ignorance is *constitutive of* the pedagogical situation Jacotot creates and not merely an accidental cause. A second answer to the significance of "ignorance" in *The Ignorant Schoolmaster* would therefore stress the *strategic* function of ignorance in Jacotot's model

   WHAT DOES IGNORANCE SIGNIFY

of universal education. In the most simple terms, it is *preferable* that the teacher does not know, is ignorant of, the unknown object in the center of the pedagogical situation, for then s/he will not impose her/his own understanding of this object on the student. What is so unsettling about Jacotot's revelation is that the Dutch students were able to learn French without the guidance of a teacher who explained the unknown object to them. In doing so, they disproved a fundamental tenet of teaching: that what the teacher does is to lead the ignorant student along the path to knowledge, gradually reducing the distance between her/his own elevated intellectual, discerning position, and the student's naïve, undiscriminating, simple mind.

Jacotot declares a full-blown war on both this conception of teaching and the understanding of the nature of the human intellect that it presupposes. The explanatory method whereby the student is led from the simple to the complex on a fixed route is, states Jacotot, a method of *stultification*. Its premise is a dualistic worldview in which some individuals possess intelligence and some do not, some individuals are able and some are unable. Explanation leads the latter toward the former. However, for uneducated students to understand that they must follow the teacher on the path of explanatory education, they must first understand that they cannot understand by themselves, that they cannot find their own way. The condition for the explanatory worldview, then, is the *constitutive inability* of the uneducated. This inability may be reduced or mitigated but can never be completely suppressed. There will always be someone, a teacher of a higher order, who may correct the student and explain that s/he may *think* that s/he understands, but that in fact s/he only believes so, and that actually s/he does not understand that s/he does not properly understand, etc. There is no logical resolution to this sequence, no point at which the regression ends by necessity, and this perpetual subjugation is what underlies the dualistic, stultifying order.

Jacotot's pedagogical method rejects the distance that is the condition of this order: the distance of understanding, which is supposed to exist between the student's belief that s/he knows and his/her *actual* understanding of this knowledge. This distance can only be measured by the explaining teacher. Instead, Jacotot postulates that everyone has the same ability to understand anything created by any other human, and the task of the teacher is precisely to compel the student to prove this to her/himself. It is here that *ignorance* acquires a strategic value for Jacotot and Rancière. If the teacher already possesses knowledge of the object at the center of the pedagogic situation, it is highly likely that s/he will enforce this knowledge and this understanding on the student. Explanation will have begun. The teacher remains a step ahead of the student, comparing and judging the student's understanding of the material to her/his own. Hierarchies are unavoidably reinstalled, and the chasm of intellectual separation reopens. However, if the object remains unknown to the teacher, then the teacher can only verify *that* the student applies her/his intellectual capacity not *how* s/he does so.

  WHAT DOES IGNORANCE SIGNIFY

Jacotot *postulates* that anyone has the same ability as anyone else, that is, the universal equality of intelligence is an experimental *premise* of his argument, not a hypothesis that he endeavors to prove. This reversal of the explanatory logic in which inability is the starting point and equality is the (unattainable) goal is perhaps *the* central operation of Rancière's book. What can we achieve given the premise – which we will uphold until it is conclusively disproven – that we all share the same intellectual capacity? Quite a few things, Jacotot argued, and the empirical effects of his pedagogical experiments appear difficult to refute. In a sense, this reversal, the understanding of equality as an axiom or experimental premise rather than an objective that should be attained, is fundamental to Rancière's political thinking as a whole. It is an idea that he has developed in many books since the early 1970s. A democratic politics, in the true sense of the word, starts from the ideal of universal equality and attempts to reconfigure the "distribution of the sensible" – the arrangement of positions and privileges that define who is included and who is excluded from a political community – in accordance with that ideal.[4]

3. This leads us to a third way of answering the question of the meaning of "ignorance" in the title of Rancière's book. Here, ignorance becomes a condition of an *emancipatory* pedagogics. At the center of Jacotot's pedagogical situation is an object that it is unknown to the teacher and student. The schoolmaster's ignorance was of strategic importance, ensuring that universal education would not degenerate into explanation and stultification. This

argument can be extended. It is not only the object – Fénélon's book, a prayer, a work of art, or anything else that can be used to compel a student to employ her/his intellectual capacity – that should remain unknown to the teacher but also the contents of the student's interpretations or translations of the object. In other words, the teacher should not demand to know how the student chooses to use the knowledge acquired. On the contrary, the teacher should also learn from the educational experience. "[W]hoever wishes to emancipate someone must interrogate him in the manner of men and not in the manner of scholars, in order to be instructed, not to instruct. And that can only be performed by someone who effectively knows no more than the student, who has never made the voyage before him: the ignorant master."[5]

The teacher should not impose her/his own interpretation on the students. Rather than merely instruct in the manner of scholars, the teacher should also learn from the pedagogical situation. Is this really such a remarkable statement, such a radical change to propose? Does it not confirm a number of established, progressive, contemporary views of the nature of a good teacher? The teacher should not be an authoritative figure who forces doctrine down students' throats; s/he should dissolve hierarchies, establish horizontal communication with students and learn with them. However, Jacotot's model of teaching does not easily conform to these benevolent views. On the contrary, it demonstrates that these views are false, and to what extent they obscure their adherence to the logic of stultification. The method of universal education does not aim to suppress authority but repurpose it. The teacher's command is crucial to compel students to exert their intellectual capacity and for verifying this effort. Consequently, Jacotot's model is also radically incompatible with notions of horizontal teaching situations. To reduce the distance between student and teacher, and to allow for direct, unmediated communication between them, is merely to reinstate that exact distance, to suppress the unknown object that ensures the equality of capacities, to subject the intelligence of the student to the intelligence of the teacher. The direction of authority, of positions of power and command, is thus a condition for true emancipation.

Jacotot's model, the ignorant schoolmaster, and Rancière's interpretation and actualization of this model a century and a half later are, therefore, powerful arguments against attempts to instrumentalize education. We should not ask *how* the student understands the object s/he is attempting to learn. On the contrary, we should actively remain *ignorant* of and detached from how the student translates the object into her/his own words and actions. Of course, this position removes us from attempts to secure learning outcomes or implement vocational education reforms. Contemporary political rhetoric about education considers learning a measure that ensures perpetual growth, a means that provides labor power to the market rather than anything associated with knowledge. In this situation, *ignorance* remains a radical idea.

NOTES
1. Jacques Rancière, *The Ignorant Schoolmaster*, transl. Kristin Ross (Stanford: Stanford UP, 1991), p. 2.
2. Ibid.
3. Ibid.
4. See e.g. Rancière, *The Politics of Aesthetics*, transl. G. Rockhill (London: Continuum, 2004), and *Disagreement*, transl. J. Rose (Minneapolis: University of Minnesota Press, 1999).
5. *The Ignorant Schoolmaster*, p. 29f.

Ignorance as Method and Methodology

Elinor Hållén

Striving to Remain Ignorant Masked
as a Quest for Knowledge
MARCEL HAD LONG suspected that his lover Albertine
may not be faithful, and he had meticulously gone over
the ways by which he could possibly find out the truth,
leaving only one possibility: read her correspondences,
the letters that she kept in the pocket of her kimono. He
would read them while she took her nap in the afternoon
and the kimono was flung over an armchair. In these letters, he was likely to find proof of an affair. Repeatedly
Marcel tries to bring himself to take the letters from the
pocket but repeatedly fails.

> And so, on tiptoe, constantly turning round
> to make sure that Albertine was not waking,
> I would advance towards the armchair. There
> I would stop short, and stand for a long time
> gazing at the kimono, as I had stood for a long
> time gazing at Albertine. But (and here per-
> haps I was wrong) never once did I touch the
> kimono, put my hand in the pocket, examine
> the letters. In the end, realizing that I would
> never make up my mind, I would creep back
> to the bedside and begin again to watch the
> sleeping Albertine, who would tell me noth-
> ing, whereas I could see lying across an arm of

the chair that kimono which would perhaps
have told me much.[1]

Why can't Marcel carry out his plan? Is it out of respect
for Albertine's privacy? No, Marcel shows no signs of
moral quandary. The reason is rather, as a passage in a
later volume of *In Search of Lost Time* reveals, he had
wanted to believe in Albertine's innocence all along.
Proust writes "the objections against my certainty of her
guilt [...] were inspired in my mind only by my desire
not to suffer too acutely."[2] This is why Marcel keeps finding objections to each of the ways of finding out the
truth, such as asking Albertine directly or having someone spy on her. Marcel's search for the truth about
Albertine's love life – a search that borders on obsessive
– actually protects him from the pain that the truth
might cause him. He goes through the motions of a
search for truth but he repeatedly brings it to a halt. This
is most evident when he stands right before what he
regards as likely proof of Albertine's infidelity, the letters, but cannot bring himself to read them. Other possible ways of finding out have been rejected as Marcel has
found reasons or obstacles to carrying them out. He is
left with nothing but the inability to go through with his
plan. Joshua Landy, Professor of French Literature at
Stanford University, comments on this passage
"Astonishingly [...] it turns out that one of the best ways
of remaining in the dark is to head straight for the light,
that a quest for knowledge may be the single most effective way of keeping our ignorance intact."[3]

On the surface Marcel's investigation bears all the marks of a rational, epistemological inquiry into the truth. But Marcel's actions are not motivated by a desire to obtain knowledge. Rather, they are motivated by Marcel's desire not to suffer too acutely and what he actually and actively strives towards is to remain in ignorance. The epistemological inquiry serves the role of what Sigmund Freud calls a defense mechanism[4], which allows Marcel to avoid confrontation with a painful fact while providing some peace of mind by allowing him to think that he has taken action to obtain the truth. Is it correct to say that his ignorance is preserved by a *method* of epistemological inquiry? Being a method it must, it seems, be motivated and strategic, and aimed at obtaining something. According to Freud, an action can be motivated and strategic without being conscious, which is typical of defense mechanisms. Marcel exemplifies this definition perfectly; since he is motivated to remain ignorant of Albertine's eventual affairs and his inquiry into the truth is a strategy to avoid the truth. But to be a method, mustn't it be consciously practiced; mustn't the agent be aware of utilizing that method? The Greek and Latin etymology of method refers to "a scientific inquiry or investigation" and "a way of going or teaching."[5] There is a certain way by which Marcel preserves his ignorance while convincing himself that he is engaged in enquiry. In this sense, there is method to Marcel's avoidance of the truth. But it is not until much later that Marcel understands his reasons for carrying out the inquiry and what role it actually plays. Thus as far as Marcel is carrying out a method it is not yet transparent to him.

The Philosopher's Love of the Perfect

The philosopher typically searches for knowledge, clarity, certainty and insight into truth. Often, this quest begins as something other, as the following translation from *Historisches Wörterbuch der Philosophie* acknowledges: "The effort to liberate oneself from error, deception, illusion and bedazzlement belongs to the characteristics of the *Denkraum* from which Greek philosophy has grown."[6] That we are held captive by our own delusions is, perhaps, most famously expressed by Socrates in the allegory of the cave. According to Socrates, the philosopher's starting-point, like everyone else's, is the cave in which he sees only shadows of reality but believes that these are real objects[7]. Heidegger's exposition of *aletheia*, originally as the reinterpretation of truth and later the disclosure of meaning, also expresses that when we first apprehend something we apprehend it as concealed and that the quest for truth, intelligibility and meaning involves unveiling appearances from forgetfulness, concealment and oblivion[8].

These examples indicate that deception, concealment, illusion and error have not been wholly absent from philosophy. Indeed, they have been considered by philosophers to be fundamental human experiences. Though such experiences have not commonly been the target of philosophical investigation. Rather, philosophers have inquired into what knowledge is and how it can be obtained. One might ask why one would not want to explore a fundamental experience such as being caught up in appearance and illusion. Why is philosophy obsessed with knowledge and truth? In the opening of another text, Landy writes about truth-seeking as a watershed in philosophy, where philosophy nearly always sides with clarity: "To judge by certain recent histories of philosophy, it might seem as though the discipline has from the outset been nothing but a staging-ground for the war of the alethophiles and the alethophobes, with no neutral observer ever giving truth and untruth an equal share of respect. Philosophy, after all, first founded itself upon the appearance/reality distinction, and has, since then, nearly always taken the side of clarity over confusion, illusion and self-delusion."[9]

Philosophy has traditionally inquired into and identified with the first part of the following dichotomies: truth/untruth, reality/appearance, knowledge/ignorance, clarity/vagueness, certainty/uncertainty, and rationality/irrationality. However, to understand Marcel's behavior, we must see both sides, that is, that knowledge and ignorance are intertwined. What first appears to be a conscious and strategic quest for knowledge is actually an unconscious (or preconscious) desire to remain in ignorance. Psychoanalysis indicates that rationality and irrationality are often intertwined since rational capacities, such as logical reasoning, often serve motivations that are not rational. Many examples of this relationship exist in Freud's case studies[10], and a number of philosophers influenced by Freud object to the clean-cut, and holistic rational paradigm that continues to dominate many areas of philosophy.

Ignorance as Method

I asked earlier if Marcel's epistemological inquiry could be considered a method to preserve ignorance. I now want to consider whether *ignorance* could serve as a method or methodology, what this could mean and what would be examples thereof. First, let us briefly consider the difference between method and methodology. While method refers to scientific inquiry or investigation, to a way of doing something, methodology refers to a body of methods and the systematic study of such methods. We use methods both in practical and theoretical work, while a methodology is a constitutive framework for an analysis of the method or methods used within a field of study[11].

In trying to understand what it might mean to use ignorance as a method or methodology, we must also consider the meaning of "ignorance." According to *Oxford Dictionaries*, "ignorance" means a "lack of knowledge or information," while to be ignorant means "to lack knowledge or awareness in general." However, ignorant also has another meaning when it refers to someone "being rude or disrespectful."[12] We might call this an ignorant attitude to separate it from a state of ignorance. When we find someone's behavior or speech rude or disrespectful, we assume that the person knows enough to be able to act with more delicacy. I want to introduce yet another sense of "ignorance," which might be called an attitude but will best be described as a reaction. In the Freudian sense, ignorance involves refraining from acknowledging or becoming conscious of information or knowledge that is within one's reach. One might react in this way to a thought or to someone else's words when it suggests something that would upset one's self-understanding or one's life in some way. This reaction often appears even before one has become conscious of what makes one upset or even that that one feels upset. Thus, the reaction stands in the way of knowledge formation. Marcel's flight from knowledge masked as a search for knowledge provides a complicated example of ignorance in the Freudian sense.

With this background, what could it mean to use ignorance as a method? Can we understand ignorance as a method as aiming to forget knowledge that one has acquired, as aiming to be in a state of not knowing, or being ignorant of something that one knows or recognizes? To consciously and intentionally put oneself in a state of not knowing seems intuitively difficult. How is it possible to unlearn knowledge? Then again, philosophers speak of bracketing knowledge. The phenomenological method, first developed by Edmund Husserl, aims to bracket knowledge or assumptions that one normally makes in perception to direct attention to the qualities of the act. For example, in the transcendental reduction, one brackets the naturalistic object of the act. One is not concerned with the object, such as whether it is there or not, if one perceives it correctly, etc. but only with the structure of the act in which we experience the object. This process does not mean to doubt or erase knowledge but seeks to methodically disregard aspects of it.[13]

Can we imagine an analogous case within artistic practice in which one brackets knowledge? Perhaps this occurs in trying not to use a familiar technique or method that is ingrained in one's painting, such as refraining from using the techniques or general rules for creating a sense of depth in painting. Is it helpful to think of this use as ignorance as a method? Would it not be more straightforward to say that one simply chooses not to apply the techniques of painting perspective? Then again, ignorance is rather descriptive here. An ingrained painting technique, such as painting perspective, must be a difficult pattern to break, which must involve constantly ignoring or undoing knowledge and competence that one would normally use in an unreflective and automatic application of these techniques. I believe that naïve art, when performed by an artist who has been professionally trained, can serve as an example here because it is typical that naïve painting does not respect the three rules of the perspective defined by progressive painters of the Renaissance[14], decreasing the size of objects proportionally with distance, muting colors with distance, and decreasing the precision of detail with distance (this can be seen in, for example, Henri Rousseau's *The Repast of the Lion*). However, naïve art also includes the work of painters who are truly naïve, that is, self-taught and thus lacking knowledge of the laws and techniques of painting. While the knowing audience may see these painters as ignorant, they themselves are presumably ignorant of their ignorance – i.e., not aware of the rules that they are breaking.

Another example of painters avoiding painting techniques that seem essential is *action painting*. In action painting, paint is often spontaneously dribbled, splashed or smeared onto the canvas, rather than carefully applied with a brush. Inspired by Jung and Freud's ideas of the subconscious, action painters, including Jackson Pollock and Franz Kline, paint spontaneously and unconsciously. Rather than aiming to depict anything specific, the focus is on the process or action of painting. The manner in which action painters paint prevents self-censure from interfering with their painting. One of the aims is to display subconscious material, such as wishes, dreams and fears, which can reach the viewer's subconscious.

The action painter, I believe, can avoid the influence of knowledge and competence by choosing a way of painting that prevents him from applying the techniques that he has learned[15]. He rebels against established norms of painting and typically has a motivation for doing so, such as preventing his knowledge, skill, expectations, and standards from interfering in spontaneous expression. He also aims for the viewer to be deeply affected by his artwork rather than to judge his skill in, say, capturing the mood of a model in a portrait. The action painter can thus be said to practice a method of ignorance in a double sense because he actively avoids the knowledge and competence that plays an essential role in both making art and judging its quality. He changes not only the artistic practice but also the criteria by which the artwork ought to be judged.

The examples of the naïve artist as well as the action painter indicate that some normative structure is required for accusations of ignorance to gain traction. The naïve artist only appears naïve or ignorant against the backdrop of assumed acquaintance with the rules of painting. The normative structure of art history and the audience positions him as ignorant. Unlike the naïve artist who has had no formal training, the action painter and professional artist who chooses to paint in a naïve style are well aware of the regulations of artistic practice. Their ignorance must be understood differently, consisting in willfully or playfully eschewing rules, such as in the mode of the avant-garde.

What might it mean to speak of a methodology of ignorance within artistic practice? Naïve art as performed by a professionally trained artist and action painting may both be said to display a method of ignorance since the artist refrains from using basic techniques of painting. We have seen that "methodology" can refer to a system of methods that are all aids in an overriding strategy. Could we regard naïve art as willfully performed and action painting as different schools of painting that are both bound by a common strategy, or methodology, of ignorance? In both cases the artist is actively avoiding reliance on specific knowledge and to use certain techniques and skills that she masters while aiming to capture something that the traditional techniques are thought to impede or conceal. As we have seen, "methodology" also refers to a critical analysis of a method or a body of methods. I will suggest that naïve painting of the above-mentioned type and action painting both perform this function. In avoiding using certain established methods and, in some cases, undoing them by the use of less controlled techniques, the established methods are

     IGNORANCE AS METHOD AND METHODOLOGY

at the same time revealed and examined. To take naïve art as an example, the geometrically erroneous perspective, the strong use of patterns and sharp colors across the whole of the canvas are the results of the refrain from using the three rules of the perspective. Naïve painting thus displays an inversion of the perspective as defined by the progressive painters of the Renaissance and so brings these established rules of painting perspective more clearly into view. Therefore, naïve art can be thought of as a critical analysis of the methods of painting perspective. Thus, the use of a method of ignorance within artistic practice has a methodological function.

We could take the suggestion of ignorance as a methodology in artistic practice as the suggestion that ignorance is *the* methodology of artistic practice whereby the arts are distinguished from other activities and sciences. Fine art is sometimes contrasted with traditional craft by their methods. In traditional crafts, methods are handed down from one generation to another often with little change in technique, but the practitioner of fine art typically relates to the dominant methods of her field critically in her artwork. If naïve art includes both works painted by professional artists who reject techniques they have mastered and works painted by artists that have received no formal training, it can serve as a different but somewhat analogous case. To relate to methods critically implies a study of methods, a methodology, which the arts share with philosophy and science. But there are important differences between art and science. Art does not strive to add to a body of knowledge, while science aims to increasing our knowledge of facts in a cumulative process through the application of empirical methods. Though there are shifts in scientific paradigms, which are seen as necessary and healthy phases of progress, not much work could be done unless there were long phases of continuous use of established methods within a reasonably stable methodological framework. The arts, I suggest, do not share these goals or motivations. Art might rather be seen as an activity that avoids relying on a base of established knowledge and methods. There will always be methodological frameworks within art, such as different art movements, but in essence, art is a creative, critical activity that will continuously examine its methods and constantly be in a process of change. There will then not be a phase analogous to Thomas Kuhn's normal science within the arts; however, what remains is an overriding methodology of ignorance.

NOTES

1. Marcel Proust, *In Search of Lost Time*, transl. C.K. Scott Moncrieff, Terence Kilmartin, and D.J. Enright (London: Chatto and Windus, 1992), C 90.
2. Ibid, F 621.
3. Joshua Landy, *Philosophy as Fiction. Self, deception, and Knowledge in Proust* (Oxford: Oxford University Press, 2004), p. 85.
4. For example, in Analysis Terminable and Interminable (1937), SE, vol. 23, and Inhibitions, Symptom, and Anxiety (1926), SE, vol. 20.
5. *Online Etymology Dictionary and The Concise Dictionary of English Etymology* (New York: Oxford University Press, 1986).
6. J. Ritter, K. Gründer, *Historisches Wörterbuch der Philosophie* (Darmstadt: Wissenschaftliche Buchgesellschaft). Band 9, s. 539. Article on *Selbsttäuschung*.
7. Plato, The Republic, Book VII.
8. Martin Heidegger, *The Essence of Truth: On Plato's Parable of the Cave and the Theaetetus*, transl. Ted Sadler (London: Continuum, 2002).
9. Joshua Landy, "Nietzsche, Proust and Will-to-Ignorance", in *Philosophy and Literature*, 2002, 26: 1-23, p. 1.
10. For example, in "Notes Upon A Case Of Obsessional Neurosis (The Rat Man)" the obsessional neurotic rationalizes his anxious cringe before Freud. For a discussion of this, see Jonathan Lear, *Freud* (London: Routledge, 2005), p. 35.

11. See for example, The Free Dictionary by Farlex,
    http://www.thefreedictionary.com/methodology
12. http://www.oxforddictionaries.com/definition/
    english/ignorant
13. Dagfinn Føllesdal, "Husserl's Reductions and the
    Role They Play in his Phenomenology", in
    A Companion to Phenomenology and Existentialism,
    eds. Robert L. Dreyfus, Mark A. Wrathall (London:
    Blackwell Publishing Ltd., 2006), p. 111.
14. For example, the fresco painter Giotto di Bondone.
15. Arguably, Dadaism and Futurism might also serve
    as examples. Both movements rejected prevailing
    standards in art.

Educated Ignorance

John Llewelyn

A man – even one very well versed in learning
– will attain unto nothing more perfect than
to be found to be most learned in the ignorance which is distinctively his. The more he
knows that he is unknowing, the more learned
he will be. Unto this end I have undertaken
the task of writing a few things about learned
ignorance.

THUS WRITES NICHOLAS OF CUSA about what he
calls *docta ignorantia* in the sphere of theology. Ignoring
theology, and refusing to have anything to do with theo-
logical ignorance, in the following paragraphs I write a
few things about a more lowly learned ignorance, educated and educative ignorance in the spheres of scientific
methodology and everyday life.

On the one hand, ignorance is a state, the state of lacking
knowledge. Ignorance as a state is denoted by a noun, the
noun "ignorance," so let us call such ignorance nominal
ignorance. Although such ignorance, like the knowledge
that would put an end to it, is a state, it is not a state of
mind if by a state of mind we mean a psychological state,
in the way belief and doubt, and suspicion and fear are
states of mind. It is a state of affairs appertaining to the
mind without being a state of mind. Just as I cannot know

that I know a certain thing, as when I do not believe that I know it, whether I know it or not, so I cannot know that I am ignorant of it, as when I do not believe that I am ignorant of it. I can be in a state of ignorance about either my knowledge or my ignorance. Here, agnotology is the mirror image of epistemology.

Nominal ignorance is to be distinguished from verbal ignorance, which is ignorance understood as marked primarily by a verb. Verbal ignorance is what people display when they refuse to take notice of something or someone. It is operative ignorance, something done. It is the deed of refusing to have anything to do with someone or something: *bouder*, as the French say, to give the cold shoulder or snub.

To ignore is at least not to want to know. But it can be more than that. It can be to want not to know. Both not wanting to know and wanting not to know may be signs of a suspension of curiosity. However, such suspension is not necessarily a sign of disrespect or indifference. A suspension of curiosity may be a sign of respect, respect for instance for the privacy of someone. We may prefer ignorance where we would find knowledge hard to bear as when we switch off a television report of an atrocity either again out of a wish not to be intrusive or to avoid the pain that seeing the pictures would cause. Because such refusal is an act it makes sense to ask after its motive. Of nominal ignorance, on the other hand, the state of not knowing, it does not obviously make sense to ask after its motive, though we might well ask after its cause. The cause of someone's ignorance might be not having attended school, having been brought up in a house without books, or having lived an extremely sheltered life . However, the explanation for someone's ignorance of a certain thing may be traceable to a more or less conscious refusal on the part of the person concerned to inquire. It may be unclear whether the explanation of this refusal should be the giving of a cause or the giving of a motive. Motives may be mixed, and in particular circumstances, motives may be difficult to distinguish from causes. This may be because we have not decided whether we are inquiring as physiologists or as psychologists. It may be because we are confused over how the hyphen in the expression psycho-physiology is interpreted, or because we are puzzled over how a patient can be regarded ("treated") as both a person and a case for treatment. However, despite the difficulty as to how these questions are to be answered in particular circumstances, no difficulty seems to be presented by the general conceptual contention that since nominal ignorance is a state it can be explained by the giving of a cause, and that if we think it will involve the giving of a motive, this can only be if we are thinking of a verbal ignoring that led to nominal ignorance, a refusal to inquire leading to the state of absence of knowledge.

The absent knowledge just referred to may be what Bertrand Russell called knowledge by acquaintance, knowledge of a thing or person, or it may be what he called knowledge by description, description of a state of affairs, knowing that such and such.

But the absent knowledge in question may be a knowing how. Knowing how is neither a nominal ignorance nor a verbal ignorance. It is a practical ignorance that is not ignorance of something or someone. It is neither what could be called ignorance by non-acquaintance nor is it ignorance of a state of affairs, ignorance that. To suppose that knowing how is either of these is to evince a certain ignorance how, to wit ignorance how to talk correctly. It is to confuse the mastery of a linguistic skill with the possession of an item of theoretical knowledge, for example with a grammarian's theoretical knowledge. The grammarian codifies the rules that constitute a grammar. But if his or our understanding of what the grammarian formulates requires a real or imaginary book of rules from which his grammar is to be interpreted, we shall have begun either an infinite regress or a regress that stops arbitrarily because we are too tired to go on or time has run out. Such an interpretation is necessary only where there has been a breakdown of communication analogous to a failure to translate correctly what someone speaking a foreign language has said to us. That is when we may need to consult a dictionary or a grammar book. Doing that presupposes a minimum of shared understanding, but this minimal understanding is the possession of a competence, not the possession of a piece of information against which we check what someone says. This is what Wittgenstein means when he says that we follow rules blindly. He does not mean that in following a rule of language there has to exist an object or objective of which we are blind, an alleged image or formula inscribed on the retina of the mind but which we cannot see. To believe

     EDUCATED IGNORANCE

that this is what following a rule blindly requires is to commit what has been called the grammarian's fallacy. To follow a rule of grammar is to behave in a regular way without there having to be before our mind's eye a principle, idea or proposition that we have to interpret and apply to make ourselves understood. Finding that we are understood is finding our regularities shared with those of our interlocutors.

The grammarian's fallacy is a fallacy because it exaggerates the importance of the proposition. It is encouraged even by that most perceptive of philosophical archaeologists, R.G. Collingwood, when he distinguishes what he calls relative presuppositions from absolute presuppositions. His way of using these expressions is liable to create the impression that he is distinguishing two kinds of proposition, whereas it is only relative presuppositions (for example, "The change of position of a hand on the dial of a barometer is caused by a change in atmospheric pressure") that are propositions, that is to say entities that may be true or false. Absolute presuppositions (for example, "All events have causes" or at a later stage of scientific thinking, "Some events have causes") are precisely entities of which it makes no sense to predicate truth or falsity. They belong to the subconscious of scientific and other thinking. They go without saying. They are unquestioned. They prescribe what can be questioned and answered rather than describing a state of affairs. They function less like propositions or statements in the indicative mood than like principles which, if they were not tacit, "understand" in the sense of being taken for granted, would be expressed as imperatives-though note that the German word *Satz* translates both the English words "principle" and "statement" or "proposition."

It is because absolute presuppositions are implicit rather than explicit that they are able to set the space within which questions as to the truth and falsity of statements may arise.

Is an absolute presupposition something of which we are in absolute ignorance? Not if absoluteness of ignorance requires that it be something unknowable for all time. Under that requirement "All events have causes" would be something of which our ignorance can be only relatively absolute, absolute relative to a certain historical span of thinking covering, say, the period from Newton to Einstein and quantum mechanics.

So, surprisingly, it is among the so-called "timeless truths" of logic, say the principle of identity "if p then p," that we should look for absolutely absolute ignorance. Timeless truths are not among what Collingwood would count as absolute presuppositions. Absolute presuppositions as described by him are not timeless truths, for he allows that absolute presuppositions can over time become relative. Absolute presuppositions are synthetic a priori. They are not tautologies or principles that lay down the analytic a priori form of tautologies. We are in relatively absolute ignorance of absolute presuppositions because they are hidden, but we are in absolutely absolute ignorance of tautologies because they are not hidden enough. If we understand them, they are not hidden enough to leave room for it to be asked whether they are true. The very of-courseness adverted to in the exclamation "Of course it is true that if p then p" is a mark of there being no room in logic to ask whether it is true and hence whether it is something we can know. So to say that we can be in absolute ignorance of the truth value of a tautology is not an admission of our not knowing. It is not the sort of thing that we can logically claim to know, so it is not the sort of thing of which it can be claimed that we do not know it. Or rather a tautology is not the sort of thing of which it can be claimed we are in the sort of ignorance in which we may be when we do not know what causes the level of the mercury to rise in a certain instrument. However, that sort of knowledge and ignorance is not the only sort of knowledge and ignorance. It may well be the case that claims to such knowledge or non-knowledge are made by people for whom the so-called truths of logic go without saying, and so, because there is no conceivable ground for doubt, leave no room for claims to know them. That is something about which there can be confidence.

But confidence is not the same as truth. Even the so-called timeless truths of logic are open to a historicity analogous to that of absolute presuppositions. For even tautologies may not be obvious to those who are learning to talk or beginning to think. And there is a sense in which the adult too is a learner, a sense in which the adult may learn something from the infant, on pain of one's claim to be judged a mature adult being questioned. The mature adult has learned with difficulty a trick that comes naturally and easily to the child. This is the trick of applying prospectively the lesson acquired retrospectively that habitually absolute presuppositions have the habit of turning into relative ones, and that even an apparently timeless tautological truth that passes for an orthodox logical tautology is ima(d)ginably revisable. That is to say, following a responsible method or way calls, in terms of the distinction made at the beginning of these remarks, for the application of verbal or operative ignorance to nominal ignorance. The state of being unknowable as determined by a currently entrenched pattern of seeing the world is an unknowability and therefore an ignorance that we ought not want to know, an ignorance with which we ought to have nothing to do, an ignorance we should ignore. But in order to ignore it we must take note of it. Put simply, the order "Ignore this" is an order that cannot be unreservedly obeyed. Otherwise put, we disobey this order in obeying it. Therefore, if to anatomize is to dissect, the act of ignoring we have called verbal ignorance cannot be anatomized. It cannot be absolved from itself. It is never absolute. Furthermore, the performative act of speech cannot be separated from the constative act of speech (since I can say "I hereby constate"), neither can verbal ignorance be separated absolutely from nominal ignorance (indeed, these two inseparabilities are inseparable from each other), for the immediate consequence of an act of ignoring is that something is in a state of having been ignored. Except that here again what is ignored is simultaneously brought before our attention, not ignored, not subjected to an attitude of indifference. Moreover, although the refusal to take notice of something may be an act of disrespect, it may also be an act of respect. It may be a refusal to intrude. It may be a letting something be, a letting be that, in the terminology of the grammarian, is paradigmatically middle voiced. That is to say, it may be neither only in the active voice nor only in the passive voice but in both or neither at one and the same time or in turns. The middle or medial voice is a voice that calls for patient listening that, when we ignore something verbally, allows what is thereby ignored nominally to speak for itself. Both right and left-brained, both *yin* and *yang*, unanatomizable ignorance is a *docta ignorantia*, a learned and learning ignorance, hence a promising hope for the increase of knowledge, responsivity and justice.

Ferrier's Agnoiology

Gavin Morrison

JAMES FREDRICK FERRIER'S (1808-1864) objective in his treatise of 1854, *The Institutes of Metaphysic,* was nothing less than an attempt to clear the ground in which skepticism flourished. Ferrier – a final figure within a heroic phase of Scottish philosophy – was at odds with the Common Sense School of Thomas Reid and sought to re-situate the foundations of philosophy within idealism. An approach indebted to his enthusiasm for Berkley and Hegel. The *Institutes* is organized into three sections: the final one of which concerns ontology, the study of being, and the first concerns epistemology, a theory of knowledge (a term that Ferrier introduced into philosophical discourse). Yet between these two sections, and notably the shortest in length, was the Agnoiology, a theory of ignorance. For Ferrier, between what there is and how it is known, it was necessary to account for what is unknown and thereby the relationship between the knower and the known.

Ferrier's conception of agnoiology was neither thoroughly engaged by the philosophical community nor did it create an impetus to generate alternative agnoiologies as a means to engage the problems of epistemology. Although the ideas of the agnoiology were not widely engaged, the philosopher John Stuart Mill[1] did articulate – in correspondence with Rev. John Cairns, 1818-92, an

Edinburgh based academic – that Ferrier's definitions appeared to be manipulated through semantic contrivance "he erects the accidental dyslogic connotation of a word into the chief constituent of its meaning, & from this definition of his own concludes that there are no other things to be ignorant of."[2] Mill's resistance to the imposition of a particular definition of ignorance can, at least in part, be seen as legitimate and perhaps indicates why Ferrier's contribution had been passed over.

It is significant how few theories of ignorance have been proposed compared to the plethora of epistemological systems. Indeed, defining the possibility of knowledge through such a negative conception as ignorance may beget a labyrinthine structure, a Gordian knot of all that is not known. Ferrier attempts to avoid this by differentiating what can properly be termed ignorance. His approach to establishing what ignorance is, rests upon a conception of the necessary relationship between subject and object. Ferrier contends that an object cannot be known without it being known by a conscious something, a subject that must be aware of itself. Therefore, the object cannot be known unless by a consciousness; similarly, the consciousness must be aware of something, it must have content. According to Ferrier, what is known and all that is knowable are unions. The synthesis between a subject and an object he termed the absolute. Ferrier restricts the term ignorance to only those unknowns that are possible to know, "all defects are possibly remediable, otherwise they would not be defects. But ignorance is a defect. Therefore all ignorance is possibly remediable."[3] This construction differentiates the unknown and ignorance. To be ignorant of something, it must be possible for an intelligence to know it. For Ferrier, this intelligence need not actually exist, it is sufficient that the deficit is only potentially remediable by a potential intelligence. In this regard, Ferrier contrasts ignorance and nescience. Nescience cannot be said to be a state of ignorance, as there is no defect with nescience; there is no remediable potential. Ferrier uses the example of boys being taught of Euclid, and learning that it cannot be known that "a part is greater than a whole" but they are not taught that they are incapable of being ignorant of this because there is no corresponding object of knowledge that is not known, that is, it is not possible to know that "a part is greater than a whole." Jenny Keefe draws attention to a similarity between Ferrier's restrictions on ignorance to exclude instances of nescience and the definition suggested by Thomas Aquinas. For although Ferrier contends that he is the first to formulate a theory of ignorance, Keefe argues that not only did Aquinas preempt Ferrier but their conceptions of ignorance, both assert that instances of not knowing and nescience differ from ignorance and that only the latter can be thought to be blameworthy[4]. That is, blame could only be applicable in situations where knowledge is possible.

One instance where knowledge is not possible, according to Ferrier, is in the ability to have knowledge of an object without a subject. We cannot be said to be ignorant of that which we cannot have knowledge. Therefore, as Ferrier says, "we cannot be ignorant of objects without a subject; and thus there can be no ignorance of objects *per se*."[5] Here, Ferrier specifically addresses the misconception of Kant in the belief that we can be ignorant of *things-in-themselves*. Whereby Kant is shown as advancing the position that deficiencies of cognition imply that *things-in-themselves* remain unknowable; however, Ferrier maintains that knowledge is only possible with the absolute and that *things-in-themselves* must, by definition, rest outside the synthesis of subject and object. This then implies not that our cognitive powers are wanting but that the subject along with the object is necessary for the potential for knowledge. As Ferrier established, that which we cannot know, we cannot be ignorant of either. Ferrier also examines the allied implication that if we cannot have knowledge of objects without subjects, then also we cannot have knowledge of subjects without objects. That is, we cannot be ignorant of the ego *per se,* as any knowledge of the ego must be accompanied by an object with which that subject is engaged.

And yet John Stuart Mill was not swayed, "the whole of his [Ferrier's] doctrine of the absolute may be thus expressed: Unless the Absolute is what I say it is, that is, unless a toothache, regarded as my toothache, is the Absolute there *is* no Absolute... The truth is, it outdoes in scepticism almost all the systems so called, inasmuch as it abolishes *noumena*."[6] For Mill, Ferrier's approach does not get started as he feels that the principal upon which it is based: all that we can be said to be ignorant of must be something which we can have knowledge of, is neither proven nor self-evident. Mill may have misconstrued Ferrier. It is not *our* potential to have knowledge, but rather it is sufficient that there is the possibility for knowledge. Yet, Mill would most likely persist that there is convenience in the formulation of Ferrier's meaning for ignorance. Indeed, he perceives Ferrier to be guilty of similar transgressions elsewhere, such as he claims that his principle rests on the conflation of two senses of the word "contradictory", that of contradictory to our intelligence and contradictory to the "laws of our cognitions."[7] Yet despite Mill's apathy for Ferrier's agnoiology, he does concede a grudging tolerance for his approach in that "philosophy will most likely ultimately use the words in something like his sense of them, so that his system serves as a mode of stating a connected set of opinions grounded in truth."[8] Ferrier's unusual, if not completely novel, undertaking highlights an area of philosophical oversight. His approach is efficient and elegant, but despite his efforts, we remain uncertain if we are ignorant of ignorance.

NOTES

1. I became aware of Mill's letter from Jenny Keefe, "James Ferrier and the Theory of Ignorance" *The Monist* Vol. 90, No. 2, Scottish Philosophy (April 2007)

2. John Stuart Mill, *The Collected Works of John Stuart Mill, Volume XV – The Later Letters of John Stuart Mill 1849-1873* (Toronto: University of Toronto Press, London: Routledge and Kegan Paul, 1972), p. 837-8.

3. James F. Ferrier, *Institutes of Metaphysic; The Theory of Knowing and Being* (Edinburgh & London: William Blackwood and sons, 1854), p. 402.

4. Jenny Keefe, "James Ferrier and the Theory of Ignorance" *The Monist* Vol. 90, No. 2, "The Scottish Philosophical Tradition" (April 2007), p. 304.

5. James F. Ferrier, Institutes of Metaphysic, p. 409.

6. John Stuart Mill, *The Collected Works of John Stuart Mill*, p. 837.

7. Ibid. p. 838.

8. Ibid.

How to Not-Know: An Essay on the Limits of Cognitive Knowledge

Jonna Bornemark

Prelude

MANY YEARS AGO, I taught philosophy at Komvux, a secondary education institution for adults in Sweden. At the same time, I taught a philosophy course for psychotherapists who were training to be tutors for other psychotherapists. The students at Komvux had low confidence in their studies; they had all failed high school. However, the psychotherapists had long educational careers behind them and were very used to being good students. I asked both groups to read paragraph five of *The Concept of Anxiety* by Søren Kierkegaard. This paragraph discusses how the consciousness and capacity for knowledge are slowly awakened. A state of an unknowing, a dreaming spirit is also described. This text is very difficult without philosophical training (even with training!), but, to my surprise, it was received very differently by the Komvux students and the psychotherapists. One Komvux student said, "I don't understand anything, but I like the atmosphere and the tone of the text. It is very strange, but yet thought provoking." These students were used to not understanding, and because I told them that this is a classic but difficult philosophical text, they were at ease not understanding it. One student said, "A stupid, uneducated person like me could of course not be expected to understand such a text."

The reaction among the psychotherapists was very different: "I find it rude of you to give as a text like this to read.
It is incomprehensible and impossible to understand."

I understood these students to be expressing a position,
such as "Since I can't understand what the writer wants
to say in this text, it is incomprehensible and impossible
to understand. I should be able to understand it directly
or it is not a good text."

Neither group of readers understood the text; however,
in the first case, this was not a problem, whereas in the
second case difficulty rendered the reading meaningless.
The text is about the dawn of knowledge and a beginning state of not knowing. I asked both groups of students to project their own states of mind when they did
not understand onto the text and see if they could follow
the slow development of knowledge. The Komvux students expressed relief in accepting not knowing, whereas
the psychotherapists were suspicious. Discussing the text
from this angle made sense to both groups, and after a
while, they found the text strange because it exhibited a
peculiarity: all knowledge arises from not knowing.

All the students thought of their not knowing as an
imperfection and intellectual defect. What I asked them
to do was instead to understand it as what James F.
Ferrier calls nescience, a state of mind at the limit of cognitive knowledge. In Kierkegaard, the dawn of consciousness includes a certain kind of negativity that calls
attention to itself. This negativity is the possibility of

possibility. That is, that which makes room for every possibility and for the experience that things could be different!

The Role of Not Knowing

We live in a scientistic society, but there is a discrepancy between the understandings of knowledge in popular scientism and (most) science. In scientism, that which is not known is understood as a piece in a jigsaw puzzle surrounded by other known pieces; there is one well-defined piece missing. From this perspective, science is asking a question similar to "what time is it?" where the horizon in question is well known and the possible answers are limited. Not knowing is here subsumed within an order of knowledge. Not understanding within scientism often creates a reaction similar to that experienced by the psychotherapists above: We should know! This is, of course, a misunderstanding of science because in science there is no end of missing pieces, of the not-yet-known. The possibility of turning everything upside down must exist, creating new perspectives. Without such a horizon, science would be dead. From this perspective, knowledge and not knowing changes place. Not knowing is not a missing piece in a universe of knowledge but a space within which knowledge can exist. Science must exist within a horizon of nescience, that is, a horizon of possibilities.

How can we understand not knowing as such a horizon? Is all not knowing not-yet-known, i.e., something that could be known if we only look in a proper way, or can we find areas where knowledge is by definition impossible? And in that case, how would such areas relate to knowledge? And finally, what difference does it make?

In phenomenology, the question of alterity [otherness or that which is not known] is central and is, for example, spread throughout Edmund Husserl's work. He starts from experience, that is, that which reveals itself to us. This experience includes not only sense perception but also structures of meaning. Mostly, these two elements are combined in meaningful sense perceptions, where meaning overflows present sense perception: For the world to exist, the "now" must be permeated by the past and future, the other person must be Other and I must be a stranger to myself. Let us consider these three alterities in turn.

1. Time

Experience demands presences of different kinds. Some presences are perceptions that our senses make present. Others are what Husserl calls retentions, past perceptions and impressions that linger. Without these retentions, there can be no meaningful experience as there couldn't be continuity, and without continuity, there would be no objects, subjects, things, or persons because all these demand identity over time. A world also demands futurality, which Husserl called protention, that is, each experience carries a horizon of possibilities that provides direction and makes them meaningful. In order for there to be knowledge, I must understand myself as a subject that understands continual objects or structures with certain possibilities. However, this very basic constitution of knowledge includes that which is not here right now, yet is present in the now. This non-presence surrounds everything known, it is underneath it, supporting it, and constituting it. Knowledge therefore cannot be complete or transparent because every focus demands fuzzy horizons.

This structure can be understood in two ways: either everything can be known even if not simultaneously or that there are always horizons beyond focus that might change once they come into focus. I would argue for the second alternative. Focusing upon a past event by remembering it, for example, always changes it: that which is remembered is not there as a "now," neither is it a retention as the memory becomes an object of cognition. The remembered event has changed its ontological status and its horizonality, which includes how it affects everything else. In this way the horizons can never be investigated without being changed at the same time. Similarly, exploring protensions and futural possibilities also changes them as such explorations always make us aware of new aspects. The structures of retentions and protensions create continuity and knowledge, but this knowledge lives in dimensions that evade cognitive knowledge.

2. The Other Person

For the world to be a world, my experience of it is never enough. We live together and the world is that which takes place between us. One person lives their perspective as it changes over time, but the world is also stretched over time. Accepting that many persons and other living beings experience the world from different angles assures us that the world is stretched beyond our personal experience of it. Without accepting the experiences of other persons or beings, there would be no discrepancy between experience and world. Moreover, without a world there would be no knowledge as there would be no object-subject structure. In order for the other person to have experiences that are meaningful to me, we must share a world, i.e., our experiences must be interconnected, overlapping and related. However, for the other person (or being) to have a related but different perspective, she must be exactly other. When I look into her eyes, I realize that someone is looking at me and that I do not see what she sees. To know her includes knowing that she always will exceed my knowledge of her. She can become an object to my knowledge, her body, experiences and stories can be the not-yet-known, which I can explore, but beyond being an object, she is also a subject, including a radical alterity to me. There is a specificity and uniqueness in the subjectivity that separates us but also binds us. In love, I embrace her alterity. I love her because she always will be stretched beyond my cognitive knowledge.

3. Myself

So, what about myself? I should at least know myself. This presumption is also a premise that western civilization has built into its self-understanding. The other person and the world I cannot fully know but there is no hindrance to knowledge of myself. Or so we thought. The problem here is that knowing myself demands a relation to myself, resulting in (at least) two "myselves," one looking and one looked upon, one that knows and one that is the object of knowledge. Are we not examining, experiencing, viewing part of the self, a kernel of subjectivity, and thus the part I really want to know? Therefore, I turn to the structure of subjectivity and find time, space, and intersubjectivity. However, the living, moving part of subjectivity is not there. Once again, it withdraws because that which experiences but cannot be experienced as an object. We always realize too late that what we wanted to know was the knowing capacity performed in every act of knowing, and this capacity cannot itself be fully known. Once again, we stumble upon the limits of cognitive knowledge. If the "I" did not have this structure, if it were fully transparent to itself, it could not relate to the alterity of the world or be open to the unknown. If alterity were not a central part of her own constitution, she would be estranged from the world.

Concluding Reflection

The limits of cognitive knowledge are not only confinements but also presuppositions for everything known. This means that an acceptance of a world, a being and life that overflows our cognitive knowledge is also included *within* any cognitive knowledge. Not knowing provides us with the space and possibility to move and makes both knowledge and reflection possible. I think it matters how we relate to not knowing. If we consider not knowing an essential part of knowledge and of being human, we can develop an interest in how it affects our knowledge and not only consider it a problem we should get rid of in every situation. Nescience also opens the gate to listening to other types of knowledge than cognitive knowledge, such as feelings and atmospheres that provide us with relations to alterities that cognition cannot.

Here, the focus on cognitive knowledge in science can generate a problem. Students and researchers are trained to understand not knowing as ignorance, making them blind to nescience, that is, not knowing as part of the structure of knowledge.

In a culture in which every instance of not knowing is reduced to the not-yet-known and thus to ignorance, only that which can be measured is considered. However, issues that evade and exceed cognitive knowledge should nevertheless be considered. Nescience is crucial, for example, to environmental questions and in respect to human-animal relations. We constantly act in relation to nature and animals without fully knowing the consequences of these actions. Nescience must therefore be a central factor to consider. Also in discussions on what a human life is, nescience should always be taken into account in order not to reduce the human being into an object!

Postlude
The psychotherapy students had many years of education behind them, and they belonged to a discipline that acknowledges limited access to oneself and others. Nevertheless, their self-image was that of one who knows, and the situation of not knowing represented an

attack on their self-image. These students were focused on gaining knowledge not relating to nescience. The Komvux students were used to being ignorant, and in this case, this actually increased their access to nescience. They experienced less need for control, and they could limit the reach of the feeling of failed understanding to remain attuned to other experiences. With additional training, these students could use this attunement to explore nescience.

An Element of Blank:
On Literary Ignorance

Andrew Bennett

THE NARRATOR IS the one who knows or, to cannibalise a phrase from Jacques Lacan's description of the analyst, the one who is supposed to know[1]. The English word "narrate" ultimately stems, through Latin *narrare*, to "relate," "tell," "explain," via *gnarus*, "knowing," from the ancient Greek stem $\gamma\nu\omega$-, "to know." There is a certain logic here: you can tell someone something because you know it. Telling is an imparting of knowledge. You cannot tell what you do not know.

And yet you can, or at least narrators can. Again and again the narrators of literary works turn out to be individuals who fail to know, who fail to know the story that they tell. And this turns out to be part of a larger question because what we mean by the term "literature" itself has to do with the ignorance, doubt, uncertainty, or with the conceptual or narrative hesitation of those that tell a tale – with what in an 1817 letter, the poet John Keats calls "negative capability" (which he wonderfully glosses as a capacity for "being in uncertainties, Mysteries, doubts, without any irritable reaching after fact & reason"[2]). It is something like a law of literature, in effect: the literary work is that which involves or invokes, at some level, a certain dimension of ignorance, what Emily Dickinson calls an "Element of Blank."[3] And why not? As Jacques Derrida, that most literary of philosophers, once remarked (in *Glas*, one of his more profoundly and unsettlingly literary performances), "you can take interest in what I am doing here only insofar as you would be right to believe that – *somewhere* – I do not know what I am doing."[4] In the same way, you can take an interest in a poem or novel or play just to the extent that you can conceive of the narrator or indeed the author as not knowing, as not quite knowing, *somewhere* or *at some level*, what it is that she is telling you. That is what one's interest in a literary work is, in effect: an engagement with an element of blank, with a certain obscurity, with nescience, with moments of sublime obliviousness or insouciance.

Although the unknowing, thoughtless, forgetful, or ignorant narrator is evident across genres, languages, and cultures, the phenomenon is particularly notable in literary works written in English and other European languages since the late-eighteenth century. It is almost a rule, a law, of Romantic and post-Romantic literature: the narrator is one who is supposed to, but doesn't, know. Examples are not difficult to find. In William Wordsworth's strangely inconsequential narrative poem, "The Thorn," first published in the first, 1798 edition of *Lyrical Ballads*, for example, the speaker or narrator repeatedly assures his audience that he knows nothing, or next to nothing, or not as much as he needs to know to tell the story that he is trying to tell. The poem is about an unmarried woman, Martha Ray, who, jilted by her lover twenty-two years ago, may or may not have given birth to his child, which may or may not have been stillborn and which she may or may not have then killed. The speaker is unsure whether Martha Ray is an infanticide because he has only observed her melancholic-obsessive behavior in the years after the supposed events and only listened to local rumors about her alleged actions. "No more I know, / I wish I did, / And I would tell it all to you," he tells us.[5] Although he insists that he will tell "every thing I know" – "I'll tell you all I know," he remarks – in fact he tells us far less than we might think we need to know and far less, rightly speaking, than he knows he should (ll.105, 114). "I cannot tell," he says three times (ll.89, 214, 243) in a telling phrase that reminds us of the relationship between telling and knowing: the phrase indicates that he cannot tell us what he knows because something stops him from doing so, while at that same time suggesting that he cannot tell us because he does not know – he "cannot tell," in that sense: he cannot tell if the tale he is trying (and in a sense failing) to tell is true or not true.

So why is he telling us? The answer might come down to the fact that this narrator is not alone in his ignorance. Although Wordsworth felt compelled to add a kind of prose prosthesis to "The Thorn" in 1800 in the form of a page-long note characterizing the narrator as a garrulous retired "Captain of a small trading vessel,"[6] far from just being idiosyncratic or paradoxical, the admittedly idiosyncratic and highly individualized narrator of the poem is not in this respect any different from anyone else. If in the end it comes down to the narrator not knowing, it also comes down to the fact that, as he repeatedly insists in one stanza, this is not just a private or personal problem but a universal truth:

> *No more I know*, I wish I did,
> And I would tell it all to you;
> For what became of this poor child
> *There's none that ever knew*:
> And if a child was born or no,
> *There's no one that could ever tell*;
> And if 'twas born alive or dead,
> *There's no one knows*, as I have said…
> (ll. 155-62; italics added)

Nobody knows, then: "There's no one that could ever tell," because in fact "There's none that ever knew." "There's no one knows" is all the narrator knows, or will tell.

Nobody knows. Jumping genres, centuries, and continents, we see the phrase coming back resoundingly in the third of Philip Roth's late-twentieth-century "American Trilogy" novels, returning as a kind of motto. Roth's *The Human Stain* (2000) is all about knowing and all about knowing other people. And as in Wordsworth's "The Thorn," the novel is about a supposedly knowing community, about a community that therefore feels assured that it can make ethical judgments about the sexuality of a young woman. What Wordsworth's poem does not quite say, because it cannot, is that *if* there was a child born, *if* it lived, and *if* it was murdered by its mother, then that murder would itself be an indirect result of the ethical confidence, the knowingness involved in a

                    AN ELEMENT OF BLANK

late-eighteenth-century rural English community's condemnation and ostracizing of an unmarried mother. What
we might then see as Wordsworth's hesitation about the
community's condemnation of a young woman, becomes
in Roth the target of righteous rage in which what is at
least minimally known is that a community's ethical certainty is misplaced. Every novel published by the Jewish-
American writer Philip Roth has been written in the wake
of and as a response to the absolute and communally
ratified ethical certainties that allowed for the murder of
over six million Jewish and other minorities in Nazi death
camps. This is part of the context for the fact that while
all three novels in Roth's American Trilogy involve severe
indictments of the condition of avoidable ignorance, they
also involve the idea that in the end, "What we know is
that, in an unclichéd way, nobody knows anything," that
"You *can't* know anything," that "The things you *know*
you don't know," as the narrator Nathan Zuckerman puts
it in *The Human Stain*.[7] Roth's narrator insists, again and
again, that in the end, he cannot fully know the man that
his book is about, Coleman Silk, and cannot know Silk's
lover, Faunia Farley: "I cannot make him fully visible,"
Zuckerman insists, "There is a blank. That's all I can say":

> They are, together, a *pair* of blanks, there's
> a blank in her and [. . .] somewhere there's a
> blank in him too, a blotting out an excision,
> though of what I can't begin to guess…can't
> even know, really, if I am making sense with
> this hunch or fancifully registering my igno-
> rance of another human being.[8]

Silk's secret is that he is a black man who, growing up in the racist cultural environment of 1940s America, adopted the identity of a white Jew. After Silk's death in a car crash, Zuckerman wonders whether Faunia Farley, who also died in the crash, had been aware of her lover's disguised identity. He concludes that he does not and cannot know. "How do I know she knew?", he asks himself:

> I don't [...] I can't know. Now that they're
> dead, nobody can know. For better or worse,
> I can only do what everyone does who thinks
> that they know. I imagine. I am forced to
> imagine. It happens to be what I do for a liv-
> ing. It is my job. It's now all I do.[9]

The task of the narrator, and of the writer (Zuckerman, Roth's stand-in, is a writer by profession), is not to know but to imagine. As an earlier incarnation of Zuckerman comments in *American Pastoral* (1997), "Writing turns you into somebody who's *always* wrong. The illusion that you may get it right someday is the perversity that draws you on."[10] To be a writer is not to know. Rather, it is to speculate, to guess, to hypothesize, to invent – to imagine – and therefore to get it wrong, and to know at least that that is what you do.

For a novelist like Samuel Beckett, this element of blank, this concerted literary agnoiology, is ratcheted up to become fundamental to the very texture of the writing itself. The page-long opening paragraph of Beckett's

AN ELEMENT OF BLANK

Molloy (1951/1955) revolves around and focuses almost exclusively on the intractable dialectic of narratorial ignorance and uncertainty. "I am in my mother's room," Molloy, the narrator, begins confidently. "It's I who live there now," he continues, with a slight hesitation over whether he is in fact in the room at all (he is in the room "now" and yet the room is "there"). "I don't know how I got there," he goes on in the first of six declarations, just in the first paragraph, that he does not know ("I don't know how I got there"; "I don't know how to work any more"; "I don't work for money. For what then? I don't know"; "The truth is I don't know much"; "Was she already dead when I came?...I don't know"; "Is what I do now any better? I don't know"). And ignorance is marked indirectly in virtually every sentence of the paragraph – with its assertions that the speaker does not "understand" or that he has "forgotten," with its multiple self-corrections and self-contradictions, its gestures of deference to authority, its seven question-sentences, five uses of "apparently," four uses of "perhaps," and with phrases such as "It seems to me" and other markers of doubt or uncertainty such as vague or uncertain verbal formulations ("There's this man who comes every week").[11]

Beckett is at the extreme end of the literary discourse of ignorance, of the anepistemologic or anepistemophilic tendency or impulse in literature. But he simply takes to its conclusion an underlying logic of the institution of literature itself. Literature can be conceived as the space where ignorance can be entertained, explored, enacted. And it is for this reason, perhaps, that the French writer and theorist of the space of literature, Maurice Blanchot, argues that what in turn most "threatens" reading is the person who thinks that he or she "knows in general how to read." What threatens reading for Blanchot is the reader's "reality," his "personality, his immodesty, his stubborn insistence upon remaining himself in the face of what he reads."[12] If, as we must assume to be the case, every literary text is individual, unique, singular, then each text will demand a new set of protocols of reading, new strategies of interpretation, new hermeneutic theories. And this is why it is literary criticism, as much as psychoanalysis, the "bringing up of children," or the "governance of nations," that is the impossible profession – impossible because in literary criticism as well you can "be sure only of unsatisfying results."[13] You cannot learn to read and you cannot teach reading if every text you come across offers unique challenges and requires a different set of skills. It is for this reason, perhaps, that Blanchot argues that reading "demands more ignorance than knowledge," that it requires "knowledge endowed with an immense ignorance" which has "each time to be received and acquired in forgetfulness of it."[14]

Like the unconscious, which according to Freud is untroubled by contradiction, literature lives with, is indeed constituted, by self-contradiction, by permanent perplexity, by ambiguity or undecidability, alongside the aporia or doubt that stems from such effects. Literature may be seen as working outside of the principle of non-contradiction posited by classical logic: it can be conceived as the space in which contradiction somehow *works,* and is put to work

– perhaps as an aspect of what Samuel Taylor Coleridge teaches us is our "willing suspension of disbelief."[15] As such, literature may be understood to be the discourse in which there is no contradiction – or in which there is *only* contradiction. *This is the author speaking*, the text asserts, *but not the author; this is true*, it implies, *but it is not true; these are people that you are reading about, but they are not people; these ideas are specific to these words in this order, but they also articulate the general, the universal, the timeless.* And literature may be seen as the space in which the paradoxical but ultimately Socratic assertion "I know that I know nothing" can be put to work, engaged, explored, performed. The part-mythical pre-philosophical (pre-Platonic) figure of Socrates wanders the streets of Athens collaring individuals (until finally his community loses patience and sentences him to death) to argue a) that the people he meets do not know that which they think they know (what "truth" is, or how to live, or what they mean when they talk about "virtue" or "justice" or "the Good") and b) that Socrates himself also does not know. Literary discourse has a similarly strange, disconcerting, dangerous, subversive function: it asserts its own ignorance and upholds the valuing of not knowing, or of *knowing* at least this one thing – that it does not know. Literature is, after all, the space of imagination, of dreams, of the unconscious. If philosophy is a "battle against the bewitchment of our intelligence by means of language,"[16] as Ludwig Wittgenstein would have it, literature can be understood by contrast as an engagement with bewitchment, even *as* bewitchment by and in language. Literature acknowledges just that language, in certain forms and in certain

uses, is beguiling, bewitching. And it is, therefore, ultimately efficacious, even truth-generating in its refusal to
offer final truths or solutions, or certainty, or wisdom, or
knowledge.

NOTES

1. *The Seminar of Jacques Lacan, Book XI: The Four Fundamental Concepts of Psychoanalysis*, transl. Alan Sheridan, ed. Jacques Alain-Miller (New York: Norton, 1981), ch.18.

2. *The Letters of John Keats, 1814-1821*, ed. Hyder Edward Rollins, 2 vols. (Cambridge, Mass.: Harvard University Press, 1958), 1.193.

3. Emily Dickinson, "Pain – has an Element of Blank –". A number of literary critics and theorists have recently argued much the same point: Avital Ronell comments that the "failure of cognition is the province of literary language" in *Stupidity* (Urbana: University of Illinois Press, 2002), p.6; Stathis Gourgouris remarks that "the way that literature thinks casts into all sorts of turbulence the status of the act of thinking, if not the actual notion of thought itself" in *Does Literature Think? Literature as Theory for an Antimythical Era* (Stanford: Stanford University Press, 2003), p.1; and Marjorie Garber has proposed that literature can be defined as "the discourse in which the knowledge of the discontinuity of thought is made fleetingly available" in *A Manifesto for Literary Studies* (Seattle: University of Washington Press, 2003), p.66. See also my *Ignorance: Literature and Agnoiology* (Manchester: Manchester University Press, 2008).

4. Jacques Derrida, *Glas*, transl. John P. Leavey and Richard Rand (Lincoln: University of Nebraska Press, 1986), p. 64R.

5. *"Lyrical Ballads" and Other Poems, 1797-1800*, eds.

James Butler and Karen Green (Ithaca: Cornell University Press, 1992), p. 80 (ll.155-6).

6. Ibid., pp. 350-1.

7. Philip Roth, *The Human Stain* (London: Vintage, 2001), p. 209.

8. Ibid. p. 213.

9. Ibid.

10. Philip Roth, *American Pastoral* (London: Vintage, 1998), p.63 (italics added).

11. Samuel Beckett, *Molloy*, ed. Shane Weller (London: Faber and Faber, 2009), pp. 3-4.

12. Maurice Blanchot, *The Space of Literature*, transl. Ann Smock (Lincoln: University of Nebraska Press, 1982), p. 198.

13. Sigmund Freud, "Analysis Terminable and Interminable", in *Wild Analysis*, ed. Adam Phillips (London: Penguin, 2002), p. 203.

14. Blanchot, *The Space of Literature*, pp. 198, 192.

15. Samuel Taylor Coleridge, *Biographia Literaria*, 2 vols., eds. James Engell and W. Jackson Bate (London: Routledge and Kegan Paul, 1983), 1:6.

16. Wittgenstein, *Philosophical Investigations* §109 (p.47e); see also *The Blue and Brown Books* (New York: Harper Torch Books, 1965), p.27: "Philosophy, as we use the word, is a fight against the fascination which forms of expression exert upon us."

Hear, Here

Jeanine Oleson

Introduction

THIS IS A collection of excerpts from the libretto for a recent experimental opera[1] that I wrote and directed, and was performed at The New Museum in New York June 2014. The opera combined written and appropriated anxiety and absurdity with catalytic objects, musicality, and was the collective creation of six actors and three musicians. The piece attempts to examine the internal and external spaces of subjectivity through language and formal means.

The libretto was written to gather language (and it's dissolution) into a situation engaging performers and audience in active exchange about the larger world reflecting on how the internal sense of Self is affected by something external to us. It asks of us to pay attention to the transformation that occurs in one's relationship to an(y) other. The libretto led us through a process that was interpretive, generative, and open over a terrain of meaning that was alternately awful and pleasurable. Once in production as opera, entire meanings and stimuli are abandoned, but reason and language arrive back in this document. Sculptures existing between function and objects become, in the opera, both symbols and catalysts for performers' actions. The largest object is a mountain on the outside, when turned it becomes a felt-lined cave. A horn is formed in the shape of the human ear; a spotlight takes the shape of an eyeball. Other objects/props include a curtain dyed with the image of an eclipse, a shepherd's crook, and clay "scores." Costumes are all similar long gowns with bodices decorated with piping based on vowels.

While texts cannot provide an experience of the performance, these excerpts are language available for contemplation and critique. This has everything to do with ignorance and ignoring.

I. Refrain
Moving Mountains Song [Six actors push and pull a black, planar mountain on hidden wheels and sing this chorus.]

Hear our ears and stomp your feet
Light our eyes and make us weep
Climb this mountain to avoid the waves
Enter into the softest caves.

We pull it here
We pull it there
Workers know
It's never fair.

Hail the eye that helps us see
But don't forget what you won't be
If your ear should speak a line
Don't expect it will all sound fine.

　　　　　　　　　　　　HEAR, HERE

We pull it there
We pull it here
The end is always
Looming near.

A dog could wag to tell you no
And you will leave them on their own
Is the cat alive or dead
It's all happening in your head

We pull it here
We pull it there
Workers know
It's never fair.

A mountain is the earth up high
A cave is space of unknown why
Land is something we believe
And what comes next who can perceive.

We pull it here
We pull it there
Workers know
It's never fair.

We pull it there
We pull it here
The end is always
Looming near.

II. Not Knowing & Belief

Curtain/Hook Solo Song [Singer enters through curtain, spotlighted. Slow, drawn out song eventually falls apart, reforms, then falls apart again. Unseen actor uses shepherd's crook to remove singer as in the vaudeville hook].

> *I don't know, I don't know,*
> *I don't know, I don't know,*
> *I don't know, I don't know,*
> *I don't know, I don't know,*
> *OH. You're here to see a show?*
> *I don't know, I don't know,*
> *I don't know, I don't know,*
> *OH. You're here to see a show?*
> *Well all the people come to see*
> *This hatred for humanity.*

Animal Consciousness Talk Show [Two actors sit with a small table between them, as in a talk show format. They nod and smile throughout. A teleconferencing screen appears behind them with a dog sitting at a table in front of a typical cityscape green screen. Dog looks quizzical at camera throughout, though at one point it puts its head down on the table in resignation. Remaining actors mill around and sniff and touch things.]

> *Actor 1: An international group of prominent scientists has signed The Cambridge Declaration on Consciousness in which they are proclaiming their support for the idea that animals are conscious and aware to the degree that humans are — a list of*

animals that includes all mammals, birds, and even the octopus. But will this make us stop treating these animals in totally inhumane ways? Teleconferencing in, our guest is Sister, a canine that we live with on a daily basis and yet, don't know much about. She's granted us a rare interview in what I hope to be a more in-depth understanding what drives and motivates her and those like her. We have Professor Dara Dahl from the Univ. of S. Florida, who is an expert on human-animal communications. Professor Dahl, thank you for joining us.

Actor 2: Thank you, thank you for having me on the show.
Actor 1: So, we appreciate your willingness to talk candidly on the show today, Sister.
Dog:…(on screen)
Actor 1: I think one of the main topics we would like to get down to tonight is whether you're like humans. Do you feel? Are you afraid? Are you happy?
Dog: …
Actor 2: The absence of a neocortex does not appear to preclude an organism from experiencing affective states.
Actor 1: Stephen Stich, a renowned professor of philosophy at Rutgers University says:
In order for something to have a belief, it must have a concept.
In order to have a concept, one must have particular kinds of knowledge, including knowledge of how the concept relates to other concepts.

Non-human animals don't have such knowledge. Therefore, non-human animals don't have beliefs. What do you think of this statement?

Dog: …

Actor 2: Do you have a concept of knowledge and the ethical impact of knowledge's comprehension?

Dog: …

Actor 1: How do you react to the statement "animals are highly emotional people with very limited intelligence?"

Dog: …

Actor 2: Do you have a concept of time beyond getting this treat? Is it linear, in the fourth dimension?

Dog: …

Actor 2: Is your desire for food a sign of consciousness or a reflex? Convergent evidence indicates that non-human animals have the neuroanatomical, neurochemical, and neurophysiological substrates of conscious states along with the capacity to exhibit intentional behaviors.

Dog: …

Actor 1: When you made a perfect ring of toys on the rug in the green room, was it a symbolic or spiritual gesture?

Dog: …

Actor 1: Okay, thank you Sister, for your illuminating thoughts as well as your deep knowledge of what makes Sister and her kind so very different or uh, similar to us, Professor Dahl. Thank you, we'll be back in a moment.

III. Plato, or, No Question

Plato [Three actors emerge from behind a curtain. Another actor lifts the ocular spotlight and focuses in on the three.]

> *Actor 1: You have shown me a strange image, and they are strange prisoners.*
> *Actor 2: True; how could they see anything but the shadows if they were never allowed to move their heads?*
> *Actor 1: Yes.*
> *Actor 3: Very true.*
> *Actor 2: No question.*
> *Actor 3: That is certain.*
> *Actor 1: Far truer.*
> *Actor 2: True.*
> *Actor 3: Not all in a moment.*
> *Actors 1/2: Certainly.*
> *Actor 2/3: Certainly.*
> *Actor 3: Clearly, he would first see the sun and then reason about him.*
> *Actors 1/2: Certainly.*
> *Actor 3: Yes, I think that he would rather suffer any-thing than entertain these false notions and live in this miserable manner.*
> *Actor 1: To be sure.*
> *Actors 2/3: No question*

Shadow Meaning [Actor turns ocular light to illuminate stage's left wall. One actor makes hand shadow animals while remaining actors eagerly guess at and grasp for words. They're attempting to remember a language. Their remembering is slow with spurts of knowledge]

Shadow:	Delivered word:
Barking dog	*TOLD*
Bird	*ACCEPT*
Camel	*PROMISE*
Rabbit	*CAVE*
Moose	*WE*
Bear	*TOLD*
Crocodile	*CAN*

IV. Re-Enactment and The Dawning Of Horror
Political Speech Choir [A podium faces the audience. The actors enact a response choir that moves from enthusiastic belief to discordant questioning. Actors move between each section to reshuffle their staging.]

Actor 1: I think it's clear from our progress today which path is preferable and which path we have chosen.
EVERYONE: PREFERABLE PATH [key of C]
Actor 1: We know that the problems we face are made by human beings; that means it's within our capacity to solve them.
EVERYONE: PROBLEMS SOLVE CAPACITY [E]
Actor2: Ladies and gentlemen, they say that one-third of the working population in Africa will die of AIDS over the next 20 years.
EVERYONE: WORKING POPULATION [C]

Actor 2: I believe that we must not stand back idly and accept this.

EVERYONE: IDLY ACCEPT [E]

Actor 1: From our use of drones to the detention of terrorist suspects, the decisions that we are making now will define the type of nation — and world — that we leave to our children.

EVERYONE: DECISIONS DEFINE [C]

Actor 1: Neither I, nor any President, can promise the total defeat of terror.

EVERYONE: PROMISE DEFEAT [E]

Actor 1: But despite our strong preference for the detention and prosecution of terrorists, sometimes this approach is foreclosed.

EVERYONE: DETENTION PROSECUTION [D]

Actor 1: They hide in caves and walled compounds.

EVERYONE: COMPOUNDS CAVES [C]

Actor 3: The reason that this ideology is dangerous is that its implementation is incompatible with the modern world – politically, socially, and economically.

EVERYONE: POLITICALLY SOCIALLY ECONOMICALLY LLY LLY [C]

Actor 3: Why? Because the way the modern world works is through connectivity. Its essential nature is pluralist.

EVERYONE: PLURALIST CONNECTIVITY?? [E]

Actor 3: It favours the open-minded.

EVERYONE: FAVOURS [D]

Actor 3: Modern economies work through creativity and connections. Democracy cannot function except as a way of thinking as well as voting.
EVERYONE: CANNOT FUNCTION [C]
Actor 1: Yes, we can.
EVERYONE: WE SCAN [B]

[refrain]
EVERYONE: PREFERABLE PATH [C]
EVERYONE: PROBLEMS SOLVE CAPACITY [E]
EVERYONE: WORKING POPULATION [C]
EVERYONE: IDLY ACCEPT [E]
EVERYONE: DECISIONS DEFINE [C]
EVERYONE: PROMISE DEFEAT [E]
EVERYONE: DETENTION PROSECUTION [D]
EVERYONE: COMPOUNDS CAVES [C]
EVERYONE: POLITICALLY SOCIALLY ECONOMICALLY LLY LLY [C]
EVERYONE: PLURALIST CONNECTIVITY?? [E]
EVERYONE: FAVOURS [D]
EVERYONE: CANNOT FUNCTION [C]
EVERYONE: WE SCAN [B]

V. The Veil Lifts, Or, Discomfort

Anxiety Address [Actor stands in center of stage, everyone else stands in a line behind her facing the audience, alternately cupping ears to listen and plugging them to silence her address.]

*Actor: Hey…hey you guys. I'm not sure what's
going to happen. When I live my life, I'm sorta okay,
but when I start thinking about what's going on,
it's all too much. I'm like, how can we survive this?
Why doesn't anyone do anything? What's going to
happen like, later today? In a month? I'm terrified
when I walk off of this stage, which I'm not really
being paid for, but that's okay actually…I'm won-
dering if the global economy will have crashed, if
the tuna sushi I've been eating is definitely high in
radiation and I'm poisoned, or maybe someone stole
my identity and spent $537 on lingerie at Walmart
that I'll spend months unraveling how to get my
bank insurance to cover. Or maybe New York will
get really bombed and I'll just happen to be I the
path…I dunno. It all seems possible. But I really
want to keep living.*

VI. Post-Apocalypse/Bliss

Kool-aid Dirge [All actors walk the stage slowly, occasion-
ally encountering one another. They move like they're
on a drug trip, like they "drank the Kool-Aid" and
believe in the blissed out delivery of language. Libretto
spoken as a simultaneous choir. All speak with breath
pushed entirely out of the lungs, sighs are long,
monotonal, and drawn out.]

Everyone
I can't believe it.
We're here.
It's beautiful.

{SIGH}
I feel so alive.
*I've been dug out of the earth to / live again in the
sky.*
Water has risen and receded
I have gone and / won't come back
We have come and won't / go back.
{SIGH}
I am not you but we are really something.
We are a multitude
We will crawl out into one
We feel / so alive.
{SIGH}
A word means no thing next to my body.
In my body it is every / thing.
The resonance bears down on me.
{SIGH}
You are we and they are me.
What were we supposed to be?
It doesn't matter / now.
I feel so alive.
{SIGH}
I can't believe it.
We're here.
It's beautiful.
{SIGH}

VII. Ending
[All actors lie down inside the cave. One actor sits up and delivers lines.]

Actor 1: Nothing can be said, there is no saying that will possibly tell about this situation. I am hunting for my heart inside of my body and talking to someone's ear. That's a problem for sure.

NOTE

1. *Hear, Here*, experimental opera at the New Museum on June 13-14, 2014, Writer/Director: Jeanine Oleson; Composers: Rainy Orteca and Kelly Pratt (aurihorn solos); Performers: Beth Griffith, David Gould, Lisa Reynolds, Sister, Diwa Tamrong, Tony Torn and nyx zierhut; Musicians: Rainy Orteca, Kelly Pratt and John Michael Swartz; Costumes: Kim Charles Kay; Lighting Design: Derek Wright.

Contributors

ANDREW BENNETT IS Professor of English and Director of the Centre for Romantic and Victorian Studies at the University of Bristol. His publications include, *Romantic Poets and the Culture of Posterity* (Cambridge University Press, 1999), *Wordsworth Writing* (Cambridge University Press, 2007), *Ignorance: Literature and Agnoiology* (Manchester University Press, 2009) and, with Nicholas Royle, *This Thing Called Literature: Reading, Thinking, Writing* (Routledge, 2015).

JONNA BORNEMARK IS Associate Professor of Philosophy, researcher and senior lecturer at the Centre for Practical Knowledge at Södertörn University. She earned her PhD in 2010 with the thesis *Kunskapens gräns, gränsens vetande: en fenomenologisk undersökning av transcendens och kroppslighet* and her publication, *The Physical sake of mystery: philosophical readings of Mechthild von Magdeburg* will be released in spring 2015. Bornemark has also edited eight anthologies and has published around 30 articles. Her ongoing research concerns Giordano Bruno; practical knowledge theory; the relationship between humans and animals; and the concept of education. She is also involved in a project on urban planning at Konstfack/University College of Arts, Crafts and Design, Stockholm.

ELINOR HÅLLÉN'S DISSERTATION *A Different Kind of Ignorance: Self-Deception as Flight from Self-Knowledge* (Uppsala, 2011) concerned the role of ignorance in self-deception and the various and intricate forms it takes. She is currently working in the project "What should a Swede know?", financed by The Swedish Research Council.

JOHN LLEWELYN HAS been Reader in Philosophy at the University of Edinburgh and visiting professor at the University of Memphis and Loyola University of Chicago. His books include *Margins of Religion* (Indiana University Press, 2008), *The Rigor of a Certain Inhumanity* (Indiana University Press, 2012) and *Gerard Manley Hopkins and the Spell of John Duns Scotus* (forthcoming, Edinburgh University Press, 2015).

GAVIN MORRISON IS a curator, and writer based in the south of France from where he runs the project gallery, IFF. He is also a director of Atopia Projects, a curatorial and publishing initiative. In 2015-6 he will be the Artistic Director of Skaftfell Centre for Visual Art, Seyðisfjörður, Iceland and previously (2007-9) he was the inaugural curator of Fort Worth Contemporary Arts, USA. Currently he is developing a monographic exhibition on the modernist architect Berthold Lubetkin for Tbilisi, Georgia and is writing a book concerning cultural continuities between Scotland and Corsica related to historical connections between those two places.

JEANINE OLESON IS a visual artist who lives in Brooklyn, NY. She attended the School of the Art Institute of

Chicago and Rutgers University. Oleson has exhibited and performed at: New Museum, NY; Exit Art, NY; Beta-Local, San Juan, Puerto Rico; X-Initiative, NY; Grand Arts, Kansas City, Missouri; Socrates Sculpture Park, NY; Monya Rowe Gallery, NY; MoMA/P.S.1, NY; and White Columns, NY. Oleson was in residence at the New Museum, Smack Mellon Studio Program, NY and Skowhegan School of Painting and Sculpture, Maine. Oleson is an Assistant Professor at Parsons the New School for Design.

SIGRID SANDSTRÖM IS an artist and Professor of Fine Arts at The Royal Institute of Art, Stockholm, Sweden. She received her MFA from Yale University (2001) and has exhibited extensively nationally and internationally. Sandström is a recipient of the John Simon Guggenheim Fellowship (2008) and the Joan Mitchell Foundation Painters & Sculptors Grant (2008). She is co-editor of *Grey Hope-the persistence of melancholy* (2006) as well as *Studio Talks: Thinking Through Painting* (2014). In 2014 Sigrid Sandström was faculty at Skowhegan School of Painting and Sculpture, Maine, USA.

BARRY SCHWABSKY IS art critic of *The Nation* and co-editor of international reviews for *Artforum*. He has published several books of poetry of which the most recent is *Trembling Hand Equilibrium* (Black Square Editions, New York, 2015). He has contributed to books and catalogues on artists ranging from Henri Matisse to Alighiero Boetti, Jessica Stockholder, and Gillian Wearing. A collection of his critical essays on art writing and art writers, *Words for*

Art: Criticism, History, Theory, Practice, was published in 2013 by Sternberg Press, Berlin.

KIM WEST IS a critic and translator, based in Stockholm and London. He is a member of the editorial boards of OEI and SITE Magazine, and writes regularly for Kunstkritikk. He has translated several of Jacques Rancière's works into Swedish, including *Le Maître ignorant* (The Ignorant Schoolmaster). He is a PhD student at the department of Aesthetics at Södertörn University, and is currently a visiting PhD researcher at the Centre for Research in Modern European Philosophy, Kingston University, London.

OLAV WESTPHALEN IS an artist who lives and works in Stockholm, Sweden.

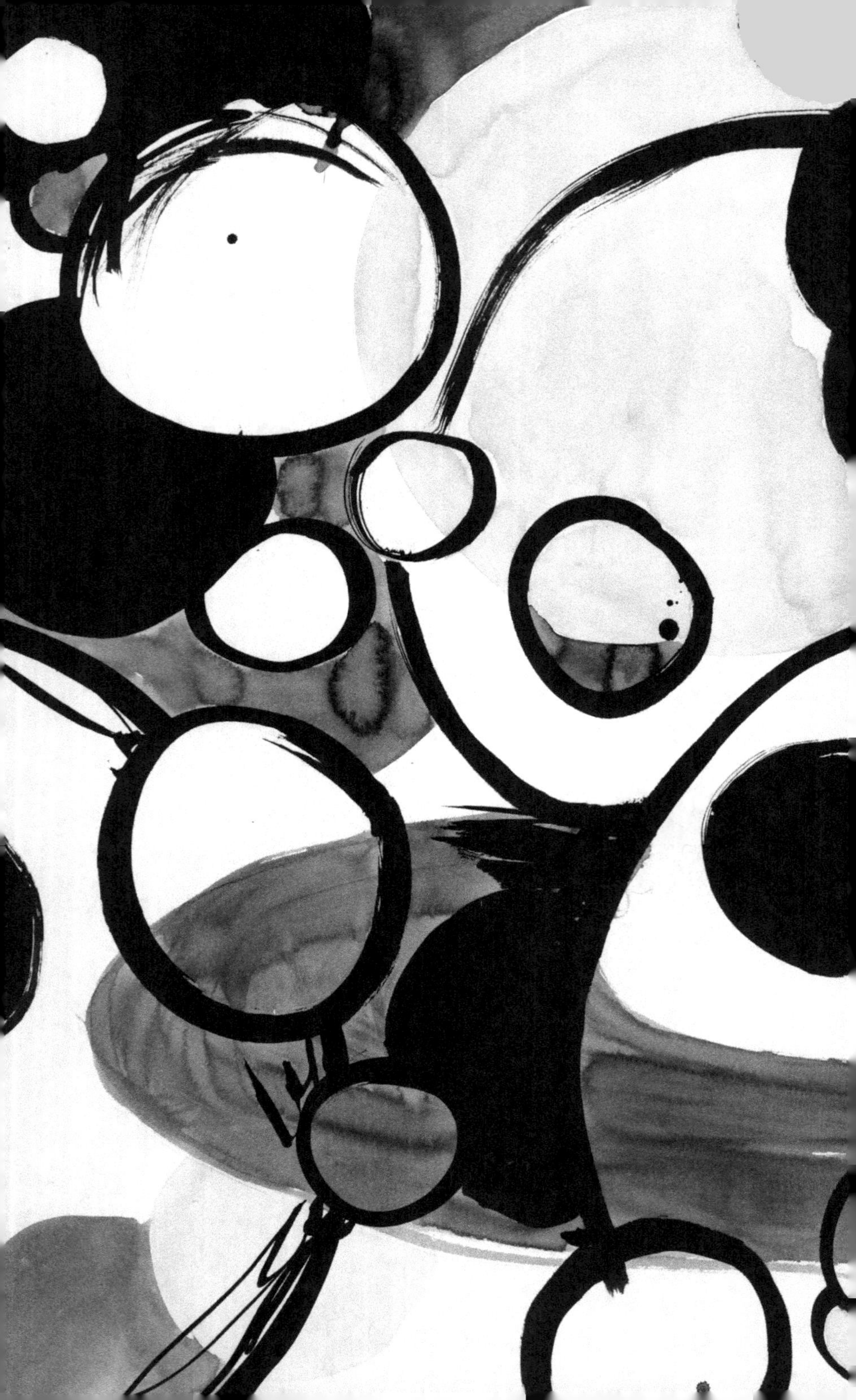

9 789186 883331